North Carolina
Appellate Law

T0381519

North Carolina Appellate Law:

A Guide to the North Carolina Appellate Rules

Pamela Newell Williams

iUniverse, Inc.
New York Bloomington

North Carolina Appellate Law
A Guide to the North Carolina Appellate Rules

iUniverse books may be ordered through booksellers or by contacting:

iUniverse
1663 Liberty Drive
Bloomington, IN 47403
www.iuniverse.com
1-800-Authors (1-800-288-4677)

Because of the dynamic nature of the Internet, any Web addresses or links contained in this book may have changed since publication and may no longer be valid. The views expressed in this work are solely those of the author and do not necessarily reflect the views of the publisher, and the publisher hereby disclaims any responsibility for them.

ISBN: 978-1-4401-4490-5 (pbk)
ISBN: 978-1-4401-4491-2 (ebk)

Printed in the United States of America

iUniverse rev. date: 6/10/2010

This edition contains the October 2009 Revisions

Contents

To my parents,
Dr. McArthur and Atty. Dottie A. Newell,
who believed.

ACKNOWLEDGEMENTS

I would like to thank my siblings, Hon. Regina Newell Stephens, Angela Newell Gray, Esq., Donna Yvette Newell, MA, McArthur Newell, II, MA, and Michael Gregory Newell, Esq., for their confidence in me and the constant love and support they provide. Thanks to Alexandra Gruber, co-collaborator of "The Survivor's Guide to Guardian ad Litem Appeals," out of which this project grew.

I would also like to thanks to N.C. Guardian ad Litem Legal Team, Associate Counsel Deana Fleming, Project Manager Kurt Stephenson, and Administrator Jane Volland. Thanks to the extremely talented Ashleigh Rose, my research assistant, for her invaluable help. I would also like to thank Hon. Henry E. Frye, Hon. Albert S. Thomas, Jr., Cherry Hardister, Elaine Mitchell, Hon. Bernadine Ballance, Hon. Sanford Steelman, Hon. Linda Stephens, Hon. John Connell, Prof. Brenda Gibson, Prof. Pamela Glean, Appellate Law Guru Frank Dail, Dean Ruth McKinney, and Prof. Charles Daye for the fantastic opportunities and knowledge imparted to me. I would also like to thank Merlot Jones and Jaz Williams for listening to me read the text aloud over and over again. Special thanks to Shea Neville for his encouragement.

In addition, thank you to family members Joseph N. Stephens, Ashley C. Newell, Mark V.L. Gray, II, Joseph N. Stephens, II, Lanier Newell Gray, and Jonathan Newell Stephens.

FOREWORD

I am pleased to introduce this long-awaited text on North Carolina Appellate Advocacy. This book will be welcomed by law professors and novice appellate attorneys all over North Carolina as a thorough, practical instruction manual on how to file an appeal in accordance with the Rules of Appellate Procedure. Existing texts are designed primarily to be a universal guide on persuasive writing and advocacy but lack specific references to the local requirements and corresponding North Carolina court decisions on this topic. For this reason, many law school professors of Appellate Advocacy have chosen to forgo the use of a text, or supplement a general text with their own materials. Practicing attorneys who dare to try their first appeal spend countless hours attempting to decipher and coordinate the rules and appendices; the violation of which could result in dismissal and subsequent malpractice claims.

Williams' text confronts this legal quagmire head-on. She places the substantive and formatting requirements of the North Carolina Rules of Appellate Procedure in a manner that is not only easy to navigate, but also simple to understand. She has drawn on her extensive experience and anticipated questions that may be asked by a student of appellate advocacy. Corresponding case references provide the reader with context; a helpful tool that law students are accustomed to using.

What a wonderful book to serve students on the first day of class and throughout their appellate career. I commend the author for her vision and dedication to this project.

Pamela Stanback Glean
Director of Clinical Legal Education
North Carolina Central University School of Law
Durham, NC
March 2009

CHAPTER ONE: JURISDICTION OF THE COURTS
Jurisdiction of the Courts

District Court

North Carolina District Courts preside over misdemeanor criminal violations and civil cases where the amount in controversy is less than $10,000. There is a district in the seat of every county. However, there may also be other court locations in addition to the county seat location. There are thirty district court districts across the state. Many counties share one district, especially the smaller and less populated counties. The district court is divided into four categories: civil, criminal, juvenile and magistrate.

Civil court cases involve cases with less than $10,000 in controversy and family law matters such as child support, domestic violence protection orders, divorce, and child custody. Some counties have a specific family court, which is separate from the other civil court matters. For example, in the following districts, family courts have been implemented: District 5 (New Hanover and Pender Counties), District 6A (Halifax County), District 8 (Greene, Lenoir, and Wayne Counties), District 10 (Wake County), District 12 (Cumberland County), District 14 (Durham County), District 20A (Anson, Richmond, and Stanly Counties), District 20B (Union County), District 25 (Burke, Caldwell, and Catawba Counties), District 26 (Mecklenburg County) and District 28 (Buncombe County). According to the N.C. District Court website,

> The 1996 report, Without Favor, Denial or Delay, prepared by the Commission for the Future of Justice and the Courts, stated, "Whether we like it or not, North Carolina's families are facing more challenges and stress, including dramatic increases in divorce and juvenile crime, which have a profound impact on our courts.[1]

---

1   See http://www.nccourts.org/Citizens/CPrograms/Family/Default.asp?topic=2

The report talked about the crowding of already-filled dockets in District Courts. "While at the same time, family matters in the courts are becoming increasingly complex and sensitive, whether it's determining equitable distribution of marital property, enforcing child support or addressing serious juvenile offenses. It is not surprising that the public, judges and attorneys all agree: the handling of domestic cases is where the courts can improve the most.[2]

After the recommendation of separate family courts in the report, the N.C. General Assembly allocated funds for three pilot programs. As of 2008, the state has eleven family court programs. In addition, some counties offer a drug treatment court that may or may not be joined with the family court. For example, Buncombe County has a post-conviction drug treatment court, where adult offenders can participate in treatment in lieu of jail time and "graduate" from substance-abuse treatment, hopefully to never abuse drugs again. Generally, there is a 50% difference in recidivism rates from those who complete the treatment programs. Guilford County has a pre-plea drug treatment program for adults. Mecklenburg County had the first family drug court, which works with parents who are in danger of losing their children due to drug use.

The criminal district court handles misdemeanor offenses. If there is a criminal trial, it is always before the trial judge only; there is never a jury. Misdemeanor offenses include misdemeanor larceny, expired car registration, resisting arrest, possession of stolen goods (depending on the value of the goods), and communicating threats. Sometimes, if the crime is serious enough or has aggravating factors, the misdemeanor will be upgraded to a felony charge.

Juvenile cases involve both criminal and civil aspects. Juvenile court disposes of juvenile delinquency cases. These are criminal cases where the defendant is less than eighteen years old and can be deemed delinquent or undisciplined. There are also juvenile cases regarding a child's dependency, neglect or abuse. Some areas in N.C. are pushing for special juvenile courts to speed up justice for abused, neglected and dependent children. For example, Cabarrus County is the first county in N.C. to offer an expedited hearing in a juvenile dependency, abuse or neglect case through emergency hearings. Topics eligible for emergency hearings include: visitation review, paternity test review, home study requests and finalized adoptions. The expedited hearings can last a maximum of twenty minutes. For that reason, they are often referred to as "rocket dockets."

---

2   See http://www.nccourts.org/Courts/Appellate/Appeal/Default.asp

A magistrate is a judicial officer who may or may not be a lawyer. The magistrate can issues warrants, set bail, accept guilty pleas and payments of fines and costs for traffic violations. Magistrate court also deals with worthless check trials and small claims court, where the amount in controversy is less than $5,000.

Superior Court

Superior courts do all that the district courts do not. Superior courts handle civil cases involving more than $10,000. As for criminal cases, superior courts hear felony offenses, with a jury. Felonies include murder, assault with a deadly weapon, drug trafficking and conspiracy. The superior court can also hear a criminal case appealed from the district court. There are eight divisions encompassing the state and the forty-six superior court districts. Superior court judges rotate among their divisions to avoid the appearance of biases that may occur with a permanent judge.

Commissions

Several commissions act in a quasi-judicial manner. For example, the N.C. Industrial Commission handles all of the worker's compensation cases in the state. It is not a court, but it can render a worker's compensation claim compensable. Thus, parties involved in worker's compensation claims report directly to the Industrial Commission, which is under the N.C. Department of Commerce, unlike the court system, which is under the N.C. Administrative Office of the Courts. Parties unhappy with the Industrial Commission's decision can appeal directly to the N.C. Court of Appeals.

North Carolina Appellate Jurisdiction

Creation and Expansion: The North Carolina Court of Appeals is the state's intermediary appellate court. It was created effective 1 January 1968 to relieve the heavy caseload of the North Carolina Supreme Court. The Court of Appeals originally consisted of one chief judge (who serves at the pleasure of the chief justice of the N.C. Supreme Court) and five associate judges. In 1969, the Court of Appeals was expanded to include eight associate judges. Subsequently, the Court of Appeals has seen two additional expansions. Currently, there are fifteen judges---one chief judge and fourteen associate judges.

Organization: Each associate judge has an executive assistant and two law clerks. The chief judge has three law clerks. The Court of Appeals sits in panels of three, even when ruling on petitions and motions for appropriate relief. Some rudimentary motions are ruled upon by the chief judge or his designee usually the Clerk of the N.C. Court of Appeals. Most business at the court is conducted in order of seniority, which is determined by either the number of years on the court or for elected judges, the position he/she filled after an election. Recalled emergency judges sit in place of retired judges or when there is a vacancy on the court.

Administrative: The chief judge appoints a clerk of court to serve at his pleasure. The current clerk is John Connell, who has served in this capacity for several years. The clerk's office consists of deputy clerks, who handle the multitude of documents coming to the attention of the Court of Appeals. The clerk's office keeps an accounting of the documents filed and collects pertinent fees. The Court of Appeals also employs administrative counsel, Frank Dail, who is an invaluable source of information regarding appellate rules and policies.

The Office of Staff Counsel at the Court of Appeals consists of the court's permanent staff. Staff counsel is made up of a director, Leslie Davis, an assistant director, staff attorneys and legal assistants. Staff counsel assists the Court of Appeals with the disposition of motions, petitions and fast track cases. Fast track cases are those with usually only one issue that has previously been decided. The cases are placed on a "fast track" and moved quickly through circulation without oral argument. The director of staff counsel also aids the court in recommending cases for oral argument and calendaring.

Routes of Appeal: The Court of Appeals generally has jurisdiction to review all matters on appeal except death penalty cases, which go straight to the N.C. Supreme Court. The Court of Appeals has jurisdiction to issue remedial writs such as habeas corpus, mandamus, prohibition, certiorari and supersedeas. The Court of Appeals has jurisdiction to hear appeals from criminal superior court cases (except death penalty cases), civil district court, juvenile matters, involuntary commitment proceedings, final orders from state agencies and commissions. An appeal from a final decision of the Utilities Commission in general rate cases goes directly to the N.C. Supreme Court.

A party may appeal to the N.C. Supreme Court as of right when a substantial state or federal constitutional question is presented or where there is a dissent in the Court of Appeals' opinion. See N.C. R App. P. 14. The N.C. Supreme Court can also review decisions of the Court of Appeals via discretionary review. See N.C. R. App. P. 15. Court of Appeals' decisions reviewing motions for appropriate relief and matters of valuation are final and cannot be reviewed by the N.C. Supreme Court by appeal, motion, certification, writ or otherwise. See N.C. Gen. Stat. § 7A-28. The Court of Appeals handles hundreds of appeals each year. In fiscal year 2003-2004, more than 1,750 cases were filed with the Court of Appeals[1].

The North Carolina Supreme Court is comprised of one chief justice and six associate justices. Their chambers are set up the same way as those at the Court of Appeals. The Supreme Court does not have an office of staff counsel or administrative counsel. It does, however, have its own clerk's office.

Note that appeals from agencies must be heard by Court of Appeals before the Supreme Court. Post-conviction appeals and reviews of valuation of exempt property under G.S. Ch. 1C are final with Court of Appeals. The only first-degree murder cases with direct appeal to the Supreme Court (tried after December 1, 1995) are those where defendant receives a sentence of death.

CHAPTER 2: APPLICABILITY OF THE APPELLATE RULES

RULE 1: Scope of Rules: Trial Tribunal Defined.

Rule 1 establishes the general scope of the Rules of the Appellate Procedure by stating that the Rules apply to any appeal from a "trial tribunal," which is defined in Rule 1(c). It reads as follows:

(a) Title. The title of these rules is "North Carolina Rules of Appellate Procedure." They may be so cited either in general references or in reference to particular rules. In reference to particular rules the abbreviated form of citation, "N.C. R. App. P. ___," is also appropriate.

(b) Scope of Rules. These rules govern procedure in all appeals from the courts of the trial division to the courts of the appellate division; in appeals in civil and criminal cases from the Court of Appeals to the Supreme Court; in direct appeals from administrative agencies, boards, and commissions to the appellate division; and in applications to the courts of the appellate division for writs and other relief which the courts or judges thereof are empowered to give.

(c) Rules Do Not Affect Jurisdiction. These rules shall not be construed to extend or limit the jurisdiction of the courts of the appellate division as that is established by law.

(d) Definition of Trial Tribunal. As used in these rules, the term "trial tribunal" includes the superior courts, the district courts, and any administrative agencies, boards, or commissions from which appeals lie directly to the appellate division.

This rule makes it clear that the North Carolina Rules of Appellate Procedure apply to both appellate courts. As a general rule, the trial court continues to have jurisdiction over the case until the appeal has been "docketed" in the appellate court. Therefore, prior to the docketing of the appeal in the appellate court, motions to dismiss should be made to the court from which the appeal has been taken.[3] What is not so clear is which types of motions to dismiss must be brought in the appellate courts only.

North Carolina courts distinguish between motions to dismiss based on procedural violations and motions to dismiss affecting a party's "substantial rights." If a substantial right is at stake, then the appellate court has jurisdiction over the motion.[4] Motions to dismiss based upon violations of the Appellate Rules may be brought in the trial court before the appeal is docketed in the appellate courts. After docketing, such a motion may only be made to the appellate court.[5]

Finally, North Carolina courts sometimes rely upon Rule 1 to hold that the Rules are mandatory and that failure to follow the Rules subjects an appeal to dismissal.[6]

RULE 2: Suspension of Rules.

It is well-settled that the Rules of Appellate Procedure are mandatory and not simply guidelines.[7] The N.C. Supreme Court has firmly held that "compliance with the Rules is required."[8] This precedent seems to be at odds with Rule 2 of the rules, however. It provides that the rules can be suspended at the Court's discretion:

To prevent manifest injustice to a party, or to expedite decision in the public interest, either court of the appellate division may, except as otherwise expressly provided by these rules, suspend or vary the requirements or provisions of any of these rules in a case pending

---

3 See Rule 25(a).

4 *See Estrada v. Jaques*, 70 N.C. App. 627, 639, 321 S.E.2d 240, 248 (1984) (ruling on the interlocutory nature of appeals is properly a matter for the appellate division, not the trial court).

5 See Rule 37

6 *See Jones v. Harrelson & Smith Contrs., LLC*, 180 N.C. App. 478, 638 S.E.2d 222 (2006) (appeal dismissed because the appellant's assignments of error fail to comply with Rule 10); *Ribble v. Ribble*, 180 N.C. App. 341, 637 S.E.2d 239 (2006) (appeal dismissed because appellant failed to include a certificate of service with the notice of appeal as required by Rules 3 and 26); *Holland v. Heavner*, 164 N.C. App. 218, 595 S.E.2d 224 (2004) (appeal dismissed for failure to timely file brief).

7 *Reep v. Beck*, 360 N.C. 34, 38, 619 S.E.2d 497, 500 (2005) (quoting *State v. Fennell*, 307 N.C. 258, 263, 297 S.E.2d 393, 396 (1982) (citation and internal quotation marks omitted)); *Pruitt v. Wood*, 199 N.C. 788, 789, 156 S.E. 126, 127 (1930) (citing *Calvert v. Carstarphen*, 133 N.C. 25, 60, 133 N.C. 25, 27, 45 S.E. 353, 354 (1903)).

8 *Viar v. N.C. Dep't of Transp.*, 359 N.C. 400, 401, 610 S.E.2d 360, 360 (2005) (*per curiam*); *Steingress v. Steingress*, 350 N.C. 64, 65, 511 S.E.2d 298, 299 (1999).

before it upon application of a party or upon its own initiative, and may order proceedings in accordance with its directions.

Rule 2 gives appellate courts discretion to suspend the Appellate Rules and allow an appeal to continue on its merits despite a party's violations of the rules. Until *Viar v. N.C. Dept. of Transp.*, 162 N.C. App. 362, 363 (2005), North Carolina appellate courts regularly allowed appeals to go forward despite egregious violations of the Appellate Rules. Since *Viar*, however, motions to dismiss for appellate rules violations have met with more success.

In the following cases, the Court of Appeals has followed *Viar* and declined to invoke Rule 2: *In re A.E.*, 171 N.C. App. 675, 680, 615 S.E.2d 53, 57 (2005) (father argued that doctor's testimony was not competent to support trial court's finding of neglect but failed to object to doctor's testimony at hearing or specifically assign error to that testimony); *Consol. Elec. Distribs., Inc. v. Dorsey*, 170 N.C. App. 684, 687, 613 S.E.2d 518, 521 (2005) (appellant failed to number each assignment of error separately in the record on appeal); and *Broderick v. Broderick*, 175 N.C. App. 501, 503, 623 S.E.2d 806, 806 (2006) (no references to the record and no statement for appellant's legal basis for assignment of error).

However, in the following cases, the Court of Appeals has distinguished *Viar*, invoked Rule 2 and allowed an appeal to continue on its merits: *Nelson v. Hartford Underwriters Ins. Co.*, 177 N.C. App. 595, 630 S.E.2d 221 (2006) (index did not detail contents of the record, but the mistake was not "egregious enough" to preclude review); *Welch Contr., Inc. v. N.C. D.O.T.*, 175 N.C. App. 45, 622 S.E.2d 691 (2005) (assignment of error did not correspond to the question presented in appellant's brief, but the appellee still had sufficient notice of the legal basis for the appellant's argument); *Davis v. Columbus County Schs.*, 175 N.C. App. 95, 97, 622 S.E.2d 671, 674 (2005) (appellant failed to specify any enumerated findings of fact or conclusions of law, but since each assignment of error referred to the same page in the record, the court had "no trouble" discerning which finding of fact the appellant challenged).

The bottom line is that our Supreme Court had not revisited *Viar* and given direction to the Court of Appeals as to when to invoke Rule 2 and when to follow the mandate of *Viar*. This lead to inconsistent dismissals depending on the panels assigned to hear appeals in the interim. Finally, the Supreme Court offered *some* guidance in *State v. Hart*, 361 N.C. 309, 644 S.E.2d 201 (2007). In *Hart*, the Supreme Court stated that "the *Viar* holding does not mean that the Court of Appeals can no longer apply Rule 2 at all. ... we note that Rule 2 must be applied cautiously. The text of Rule 2 provides two instances in which an appellate court may waive compliance with the appellate rules: (1) '[t]o prevent manifest injustice to a party;' and (2) 'to expedite decision in the public interest.'" Nonetheless, the appellate courts seem to invoke Rule 2 at will without a discussion of manifest injustice or public interest, particularly at the Court of Appeals.[9] See Rules 3 and 3.1 below.

Consequently, there is no clear rule on when dismissal is required due to an appellate rule violation, except in violations which result in no appellate jurisdiction and interlocutory appeals. Specifically, in Rule 3.1, expedited appeals in juvenile cases, the appellate court does not have jurisdiction to hear a case where a parent failed to sign the notice of appeal. An interlocutory order not is appealable because it is one made during the pendency of an action, which does not dispose of the case, but leaves it for further action by the trial court in order to settle and determine the entire controversy.[10] Generally, a party cannot immediately appeal from an interlocutory order unless failure to grant immediate review would affect a substantial right under N.C. Gen. Stat. §§ 1-277 and 7A-27(d).

Thus, a party may appeal an interlocutory order under two circumstances: (1) if the trial court certifies that there is no just reason to delay the appeal after it enters a final judgment as to fewer than all of the claims or parties in an action; or (2) if the order affects a substantial right claimed by the appellant and may prejudice the appellant if the appeal is not heard before the final judgment is issued.[11] The appellate courts have found that certain issues automatically affect substantial rights, including jurisdiction, promoting judicial economy and the dismissal of a claim under summary judgment.[12]

Note that even when an appellant is entitled to appeal an interlocutory order, the appellant is not required to do so.[13] "The reason for these rules is to prevent fragmentary, premature and unnecessary appeals by permitting the trial divisions to have done with a case fully and finally before it is presented to the appellate division."[14]

---

9   *See State v. Denny*, 179 N.C. App. 822, 635 S.E.2d 438 (2006), *affirmed in part, modified in part, reversed by, in part,* 361 N.C. 662, 652 S.E.2d 212 (2007); *State v. Holt*, 181 N.C. App. 328, 639 S.E.2d 65 (2007); *Nelson v. Hartford Underwriters Ins. Co.*, 177 N.C. App. 595, 630 S.E.2d 221 (2006).

10   *Veazey v. City of Durham*, 231 N.C. 357, 362, 57 S.E.2d 377, 381 (1950).

11   *Dep't of Transp. v. Rowe*, 351 N.C. 172, 174-75, 521 S.E.2d 707, 709 (1999) (quoting *Veazey*, 231 N.C. at 362, 57 S.E.2d at 381); *see also Pelican Watch v. U.S. Fire Ins. Co.*, 323 N.C. 700, 702, 375 S.E.2d 161, 162 (1989).

12   *See Harris v. Matthews*, 361 N.C. 265, 643 S.E.2d 566 (2007); *Davis v. Davis*, 360 N.C. 518, 631 S.E.2d 114 (2006); *Tinch v. Video Indus. Servs.*, 347 N.C. 380, 382, 493 S.E.2d 426, 428 (1997).

13   *Dep't of Transp. v. Rowe*, 351 N.C. at 176, 521 S.E.2d at 710.

14   *Waters v. Qualified Personnel, Inc.*, 294 N.C. 200, 207, 240 S.E.2d 338, 343 (1978).

RULE 3: Appeal in Civil Cases—How and When Taken.

(a) Filing the Notice of Appeal. Any party entitled by law to appeal from a judgment or order of a superior or district court rendered in a civil action or special proceeding may take appeal by filing notice of appeal with the clerk of superior court and serving copies thereof upon all other parties within the time prescribed by subsection (c) of this rule.

(b) Special Provisions. Appeals in the following types of cases shall be taken in the time and manner set out in the General Statutes and appellate rules sections noted:

(1) Juvenile matters pursuant to N.C.G.S. § 7B-2602; the identity of persons under the age of eighteen at the time of the proceedings in the trial division shall be protected pursuant to Rule 3.1(b).

(2) Appeals pursuant to N.C.G.S. § 7B-1001 shall be subject to the provisions of Rule 3.1.

(c) Time for Taking Appeal. In civil actions and special proceedings, a party must file and serve a notice of appeal:

(1) within thirty days after entry of judgment if the party has been served with a copy of the judgment within the three day period prescribed by Rule 58 of the Rules of Civil Procedure; or

(2) within thirty days after service upon the party of a copy of the judgment if service was not made within that three day period; provided that

(3) if a timely motion is made by any party for relief under Rules 50(b), 52(b) or 59 of the Rules of Civil Procedure, the thirty day period for taking appeal is tolled as to all parties until entry of an order disposing of the motion and then runs as to each party from the date of entry of the order or its untimely service upon the party, as provided in subdivisions (1) and (2) of this subsection (c). In computing the time for filing a notice of appeal, the provision for additional time after service by mail in Rule 27(b) of these rules and Rule 6(e) of the N.C. Rules of Civil Procedure shall not apply.

If timely notice of appeal is filed and served by a party, any other party may file and serve a notice of appeal within ten days after the first notice of appeal was served on such party.

(d) Content of Notice of Appeal. The notice of appeal required to be filed and served by subsection (a) of this rule shall specify the party or parties taking the appeal; shall designate the judgment or order from which appeal is taken and the court to which appeal is taken; and shall be signed by counsel of record for the party or parties taking the appeal, or by any such party not represented by counsel of record.

(e) Service of Notice of Appeal. Service of copies of the notice of appeal may be made as provided in Rule 26.

Note that Rule 3 describes the process and time limits for filing notice of appeal. However, Rule 3(b) specifically exempts juvenile cases from the general procedure. Instead, GAL attorneys must comply with the statutory timelines set out in N.C. Gen. Stat. § 7B-1001 and the new Appellate Rule 3.1, discussed below.

RULE 3.1: Appeal in Qualifying Juvenile Cases—How and When Taken; Special Rules.

(a) Filing the Notice of Appeal. Any party entitled by law to appeal from a trial court judgment or order rendered in a case involving termination of parental rights and issues of juvenile dependency or juvenile abuse and/or neglect, appealable pursuant to N.C.G.S. § 7B-1001, may take appeal by filing notice of appeal with the clerk of superior court and serving copies thereof upon all other parties in the time and manner set out in Chapter 7B of the General Statutes of North Carolina. Trial counsel or an appellant not represented by counsel shall be responsible for filing and serving the notice of appeal in the time and manner required. If the appellant is represented by counsel, both the trial counsel and appellant must sign the notice of appeal, and the appellant shall cooperate with counsel throughout the appeal. All such appeals shall comply with the provisions set out in subsection (b) of this rule and, except as hereinafter provided by this rule, all other existing Rules of Appellate Procedure shall remain applicable.

(b) Protecting the Identity of Juveniles. For appeals filed pursuant to this rule and for extraordinary writs filed in cases to which this rule applies, the identity of involved persons under the age of eighteen at the time of the proceedings in the trial division (covered juveniles) shall be referenced only by the use of initials or pseudonyms in briefs, petitions, and all other filings, and shall be similarly redacted from all documents, exhibits, appendixes, or arguments submitted with such filings. If the parties desire to use pseudonyms, they shall stipulate in the record on appeal to the pseudonym to be used for each covered juvenile. Courts of the appellate division are not bound by the stipulation, and case captions will utilize initials. Further, the addresses and social security numbers of all covered juveniles shall be excluded from all filings and documents, exhibits, appendixes, and arguments. In cases subject to this rule, the first document filed in the appellate courts and the record on appeal shall contain the notice required by Rule 9(a).

The substitution and redaction requirements of this rule shall not apply to settled records on appeal; supplements filed pursuant to Rule 11(c); objections, amendments, or proposed alternative records on appeal submitted pursuant to Rule 3.1(c)(2); and any verbatim transcripts submitted pursuant to Rule 9(c). Pleadings and filings not subject to substitution and redaction requirements shall include the following notice on the first page of the document immediately underneath the title and in uppercase typeface: FILED PURSUANT TO RULE [3(b)(1)] [3.1(b)] [4(e)]; SUBJECT TO PUBLIC INSPECTION ONLY BY ORDER OF A COURT OF THE APPELLATE DIVISION.

Filings in cases governed by this rule that are not subject to substitution and redaction requirements will not be published on the Court's electronic filing site and will be available to the public only with the permission of a court of the appellate division. In addition, the juvenile's address and social security number shall be excluded from all filings, documents, exhibits, or arguments with the exception of sealed verbatim transcripts submitted pursuant to Rule 9(c).

(c) Expediting Filings. Appeals filed pursuant to these provisions shall adhere strictly to the expedited procedures set forth below:

(1) Transcripts. Within one business day after the notice of appeal has been filed, the clerk of superior court shall notify the court reporting coordinator of the Administrative Office of the Courts of the date the notice of appeal was filed and the names of the parties to the appeal and their respective addresses or addresses of their counsel. Within two business days of receipt of such

notification, the court reporting coordinator shall assign a transcriptionist to the case.

When there is an order establishing the indigency of the appellant, the transcriptionist shall prepare and deliver a transcript of the designated proceedings to the appellant and provide copies to the office of the clerk of the Court of Appeals and to the respective parties to the appeal at the addresses provided within thirty-five days from the date of assignment.

When there is no order establishing the indigency of the appellant, the appellant shall have ten days from the date that the transcriptionist is assigned to make written arrangements with the assigned transcriptionist for the production and delivery of the transcript of the designated proceedings. If such written arrangement is made, the transcriptionist shall prepare and deliver a transcript of the designated proceedings to the appellant and provide copies to the office of the clerk of the Court of Appeals and to the respective parties to the appeal at the addresses provided within forty-five days from the date of assignment. The non-indigent appellant shall bear the cost of the appellant's copy of the transcript.

When there is no order establishing the indigency of the appellee, the appellee shall bear the cost of receiving a copy of the requested transcript.

Motions for extensions of time to prepare and deliver transcripts are disfavored and will not be allowed by the Court of Appeals absent extraordinary circumstances.

(2) Record on Appeal. Within ten days after receipt of the transcript, the appellant shall prepare and serve upon all other parties a proposed record on appeal constituted in accordance with Rule 9. Trial counsel for the appealing party shall have a duty to assist appellate counsel, if separate counsel is appointed or retained for the appeal, in preparing and serving a proposed record on appeal. Within ten days after service of the proposed record on appeal upon an appellee, the appellee may serve upon all other parties:
1. a notice of approval of the proposed record;

2. specific objections or amendments to the proposed record on appeal, or

3. a proposed alternative record on appeal.

If the parties agree to a settled record on appeal within twenty days after receipt of the transcript, the appellant shall file three legible copies of the settled record on appeal in the office of the clerk of the Court of Appeals within five business days from the date the record was settled. If all appellees fail within the times allowed them either to serve notices of approval or to serve objections, amendments, or proposed alternative records on appeal, the appellant's proposed record on appeal shall constitute the settled record on appeal, and the appellant shall file three legible copies thereof in the office of the clerk of the Court of Appeals within five business days from the last date upon which any appellee could have served such objections, amendments, or proposed alternative record on appeal. If an appellee timely serves amendments, objections, or a proposed alternative record on appeal and the parties cannot agree to the settled record within thirty days after receipt of the transcript, each party shall file three legible copies of the following documents in the office of the clerk of the Court of Appeals within five business days after the last day upon which the record can be settled by agreement:

1. the appellant shall file his or her proposed record on appeal, and

2. an appellee shall file his or her objections, amendments, or proposed alternative record on appeal.

No counsel who has appeared as trial counsel for any party in the proceeding shall be permitted to withdraw, nor shall such counsel be otherwise relieved of any responsibilities imposed pursuant to this rule, until the record on appeal has been filed in the office of the clerk of the Court of Appeals as provided herein.

(3) Briefs. Within thirty days after the record on appeal has been filed with the Court of Appeals, the appellant shall file his or her brief in the office of the clerk of the Court of Appeals and serve copies upon all other parties of record. Within thirty days after the appellant's brief has been served on an appellee, the appellee shall file his or her brief in the office of the clerk of the Court of Appeals and serve copies upon all other parties of record. Motions for extensions of time to file briefs will not be allowed absent extraordinary circumstances.

(d) No-Merit Briefs. In an appeal taken pursuant to N.C.G.S. § 7B-1001, if, after a conscientious and thorough review of the record on appeal, appellate counsel concludes that the record contains no issue of merit on which to base an argument for relief and that the appeal would be frivolous, counsel may file a no-merit brief. In the brief, counsel shall identify any issues in the record on appeal that might arguably support the appeal and shall state why those issues lack merit or would not alter the ultimate result. Counsel shall provide the appellant with a copy of the no-merit brief, the transcript, the record on appeal, and any Rule 11(c) supplement or exhibits that have been filed with the appellate court. Counsel shall also advise the appellant in writing that the appellant has the option of filing a pro se brief within thirty days of the date of the filing of the no-merit brief and shall attach to the brief evidence of compliance with this subsection.

(e) Calendaring Priority. Appeals filed pursuant to this rule will be given priority over other cases being considered by the Court of Appeals and will be calendared in accordance with a schedule promulgated by the Chief Judge. Unless otherwise ordered by the Court of Appeals, cases subject to the expedited procedures set forth in this rule shall be disposed of on the record and briefs and without oral argument.

The new Rule 3.1 (formerly Rule 3A) shortens the length of GAL appeals by a year or more, marking a major step forward in expediting permanency for the children GAL represents. GAL attorneys should pay particular attention to Rule 3.1's two most important timesaving features: production of the transcript under Rule 3.1(b)(1) and of the record on appeal under Rule 3.1(b)(2). Note that the Appellant Party must sign the Notice of Appeal, or the appellate court will have no subject matter jurisdiction.[15]

Additionally, it is common practice for lawyers to use pseudonyms for children instead of their initials for ease of reading. Under Rule 3.1(b), the parties now have to stipulate to the pseudonym, if there will be one, in the record. Thus, the briefs will all have the same name/initials. Further, before the new rules were enacted, the juvenile's name always had to be redacted from the record and other filed documents. Now, however, there are documents which are not subject to redaction (such as sealed records). These documents may be filed with the mandatory notice on the first page.

---

15   *In re L.B.* 187 N.C. App. 326, 331, 653 S.E.2d 240, 244 (2007).

Under Rule 3.1(b)(1), the AOC Court Reporting Coordinator assigns the transcriptionist to the appeal. The transcriptionist must then deliver the transcript within 35 days to both parties and the Court of Appeals. Any motions for extension of time to complete the transcript are now filed in the Court of Appeals, rather than in the trial court. Although this requirement is not clearly stated in Rule 3.1, it is implied in the text of the Rule. The Court of Appeals has, by ruling on such motions to extend even though the appeal has not yet been docketed in the Court, acknowledged this requirement. Motions to extend the time to produce the transcript are filed by counsel for appellants, not the transcriptionist.

Rule 3.1(c)(1) requires an order of indigency of the appellant, which clarifies who pays the cost of the transcript, prior to the production and service of the transcript. Rule 3.1(b)(2) requires the appellant to serve the proposed record on appeal upon all other parties on appeal within 10 days after receiving the transcript. These parties must then submit any objections to the proposed record within 10 days of receiving it from the appellant. If the parties agree to the settled record within 20 days after the appellant received the transcript, or if the appellee serves neither notice of approval nor objection to the proposed record, then the duty falls on the appellant to file three copies of the record with the Court of Appeals. However, if the parties cannot agree to a settled record within 30 days after the appellant's receipt of the transcript, then the appellant must file the proposed record, and the appellee must file any objections or amendments or the proposed alternative record on appeal.

The rule speeds up the appeals process in two other provisions. First, absent extraordinary circumstances, the court will not grant extensions of time to prepare the transcript, record and briefs. In the past, these areas led to huge delays. Also, Rule 3.1 gives "calendaring priority" to GAL cases. Unless otherwise ordered by the Court of Appeals, the rule limits cases to being heard only on the record and briefs – without oral argument.

The briefing schedule remains essentially the same as it was under Rule 3, with one important exception. Under Rule 3.1(b)(3), the appellant's brief is due within 30 days after the settled record has been filed with the appellate court. In the past, the date the record was mailed to the parties triggered the 30-day briefing schedule. Rule 3.1 requires that both the appellant and the appellant's attorney sign the notice of appeal. The rule also prohibits trial counsel from withdrawing from the case until the record has been filed with the appellate court.

A new provision for no-merit briefs was added to the rules in response to appointed attorneys for the indigent, who could find no merit for a reversal of the trial court's determination. The no-merit briefs are treated the same as Anders briefs.

CHAPTER THREE: FILING AN APPEAL

In criminal cases, the appellant has fourteen days after the judgment is entered to file a notice of appeal, or appeal orally at the conclusion of the trial. See Rule 4 below:

RULE 4: Appeal In Criminal Cases—How And When Taken.

(a) Manner and Time. Any party entitled by law to appeal from a judgment or order of a superior or district court rendered in a criminal action may take appeal by

(1) giving oral notice of appeal at trial, or

(2) filing notice of appeal with the clerk of superior court and serving copies thereof upon all adverse parties within fourteen days after entry of the judgment or order or within fourteen days after a ruling on a motion for appropriate relief made during the fourteen day period following entry of the judgment or order. Appeals from district court to superior court are governed by N.C.G.S. §§ 15A-1431 and -1432.

(b) Content of Notice of Appeal. The notice of appeal required to be filed and served by subdivision (a)(2) of this rule shall specify the party or parties taking the appeal; shall designate the judgment or order from which appeal is taken and the court to which appeal is taken; and shall be signed by counsel of record for the party or parties taking the appeal, or by any such party not represented by counsel of record.

(c) Service of Notice of Appeal. Service of copies of the notice of appeal may be made as provided in Rule 26.

(d) To Which Appellate Court Addressed. An appeal of right from a judgment of a superior court by any person who has been convicted of murder in the first degree and sentenced to death shall be filed in the Supreme Court. In all other criminal cases, appeal shall be filed in the Court of Appeals.

(e) Protecting the Identity of Juvenile Victims of Sexual Offenses. For appeals filed pursuant to this rule and for extraordinary writs filed in cases to which this rule applies, the identities of all victims of sexual offenses the trial court record shows were under the age of eighteen when the trial division proceedings occurred, including documents or other materials concerning delinquency proceedings in district court, shall be protected pursuant to Rule 3.1(b).

Rules 3 and 3.1, *supra*, govern the timing of civil and juvenile appeals. The content of the notice of appeal is simple; all that is needed is a caption with the case name and file number, the party who is appealing, which order is being appealed and a signature of the appellant's attorney, unless the appellate is proceeding *pro se*. Notices of appeal must be served on all the parties just like all other pleadings.[16]

---

16   *See* Rules 4 and 5 of the N.C. Rules of Civil Procedure.

CHAPTER FOUR: WHO CAN APPEAL?

Generally, any party to the action may file an appeal. Parties may intervene or act jointly during the pendency of the appeal.[17] Under Rule 5, separate parties could join as one party to defend or prosecute an appeal. Most parties prefer to remain an independent party to an appeal. Should parties agree to collaborate with each other in filing one appellee brief, such collaboration does not require joinder of parties.

However, joinder has its benefits. For instance, joint appellants share the increased workload that comes with filing the appeal, such as requesting the transcript and compiling the proposed record. Joinder of appellants also shows the court a unified front standing opposed to a trial court order. But if parties decide to join, they must establish good communication and share documents and other information in a timely manner. See Rule 5 below:

RULE 5: Joinder of Parties On Appeal.

(a) Appellants. If two or more parties are entitled to appeal from a judgment, order, or other determination and their interests are such as to make their joinder in appeal practicable, they may file and serve a joint notice of appeal in accordance with Rules 3 and 4; or they may join in appeal after timely taking of separate appeals by filing notice of joinder in the office of the clerk of superior court and serving copies thereof upon all other parties, or in a criminal case they may give a joint oral notice of appeal.

(b) Appellees. Two or more appellees whose interests are such as to make their joinder on appeal practicable may, by filing notice of joinder in the office of the clerk of superior court and serving copies thereof upon all other parties, so join.

---

17   *Taylor v. Abernethy*, 149 N.C. App. 263, 268, 560 S.E.2d 233, 236 (2002), *disc. rev. denied*, 356 N.C. 695, 579 S.E.2d 102 (2003).

(c) Procedure after Joinder. After joinder, the parties proceed as a single appellant or appellee. Filing and service of papers by and upon joint appellants or appellees is as provided by Rule 26(e).

Rule 6 is discussed in Chapter Twelve regarding costs.

CHAPTER FIVE: THE TRANSCRIPT

As discussed earlier in this manual, Rule 3.1 makes Rule 7's timing requirements inapplicable to juvenile cases. However, Rule 7 may be invoked on other issues. For instance, Rule 7(a)(1) states that if the appellant argues on appeal that a finding or conclusion of the trial court is unsupported by or contrary to the evidence, the appellant must file with the record on appeal a transcript of all evidence relevant to such a finding or conclusion.[18] Without evidence in the record, the appellate court won't assume error by the trial judge.[19] In addition, Rule 7(b)(3) requires that a neutral person[20] – not a relative or employee of any of the parties – prepare the transcript, unless the parties agree by stipulation.

RULE 7: Preparation of The Transcript; Court Reporter's Duties.

(a) Ordering the Transcript.

(1) Civil Cases. Within fourteen days after filing the notice of appeal the appellant shall contract for the transcription of the proceedings or of such parts of the proceedings not already on file, as the appellant deems necessary, in accordance with these rules, and shall provide the following information in writing: a designation of the parts of the proceedings to be transcribed; the name and address of the court reporter or other neutral person designated to prepare the transcript; and, where portions of the proceedings have been designated to be transcribed, a statement of the issues the appellant intends to raise on appeal. The appellant shall file the written documentation of this transcript contract with the clerk of the trial tribunal, and serve a copy of it upon all other parties of record and upon the person designated to prepare the transcript. If

---

18   *State v. Berryman*, 360 N.C. 209, 624 S.E.2d 350 (2006).

19   *See Faulkenberry v. Faulkenberry*, 169 N.C. App. 428, 430, 610 S.E.2d 237, 239 (2005) (mother's failure to submit factual record under Rule 7(a)(1) gave the court no basis for reversing findings that mother's adulterous relationship placed undue stress on children).

20   *See Spencer v. Spencer*, 156 N.C. App. 1, 575 S.E.2d 780 (2003).

the appellant intends to urge on appeal that a finding or conclusion of the trial court is unsupported by the evidence or is contrary to the evidence, the appellant shall cite in the record on appeal the volume number, page number, and line number of all evidence relevant to such finding or conclusion. If an appellee deems a transcript of other parts of the proceedings to be necessary, the appellee, within fourteen days after the service of the written documentation of the appellant, shall contract for the transcription of any additional parts of the proceedings or such parts of the proceedings not already on file, in accordance with these rules. The appellee shall file with the clerk of the trial tribunal, and serve on all other parties of record, written documentation of the additional parts of the proceedings to be transcribed and the name and address of the court reporter or other neutral person designated to prepare the transcript.

In civil cases and special proceedings where there is an order establishing the indigency of a party entitled to appointed appellate counsel, the ordering of the transcript shall be as in criminal cases where there is an order establishing the indigency of the defendant as set forth in Rule 7(a)(2).

(2) Criminal Cases. In criminal cases where there is no order establishing the indigency of the defendant for the appeal, the defendant shall contract for the transcription of the proceedings as in civil cases.

When there is an order establishing the indigency of the defendant, unless the trial judge's appeal entries specify or the parties stipulate that parts of the proceedings need not be transcribed, the clerk of the trial tribunal shall order a transcript of the proceedings by serving the following documents upon either the court reporter(s) or neutral person designated to prepare the transcript: a copy of the appeal entries signed by the judge; a copy of the trial court's order establishing indigency for the appeal; and a statement setting out the name, address, telephone number and e-mail address of appellant's counsel. The clerk shall make an entry of record reflecting the date these documents were served upon the court reporter(s) or transcriptionist.

(b) Production and Delivery of Transcript.

(1) Production. In civil cases: from the date the requesting party serves the written documentation of the transcript contract on the person designated to prepare the transcript, that person shall have sixty days to prepare and electronically deliver the transcript.

In criminal cases where there is no order establishing the indigency of the defendant for the appeal: from the date the requesting party serves the written documentation of the transcript contract upon the person designated to prepare the transcript, that person shall have sixty days to produce and electronically deliver the transcript in non-capital cases and one hundred twenty days to produce and electronically deliver the transcript in capitally tried cases.

In criminal cases where there is an order establishing the indigency of the defendant for the appeal: from the date listed on the appeal entries as the "Date order delivered to transcriptionist," that person shall have sixty-five days to produce and electronically deliver the transcript in non-capital cases and one hundred twenty-five days to produce and electronically deliver the transcript in capitally tried cases.

The transcript format shall comply with Appendix B of these rules.

Except in capitally tried criminal cases which result in the imposition of a sentence of death, the trial tribunal, in its discretion and for good cause shown by the appellant, may extend the time to produce the transcript for an additional thirty days. Any subsequent motions for additional time required to produce the transcript may only be made to the appellate court to which appeal has been taken. All motions for extension of time to produce the transcript in capitally tried cases resulting in the imposition of a sentence of death shall be made directly to the Supreme Court by the appellant.

(2) Delivery. The court reporter, or person designated to prepare the transcript, shall electronically deliver the completed transcript, with accompanying PDF disk to the parties including the district attorney and Attorney General of North Carolina in criminal cases, as ordered, within the time provided by this rule, unless an extension of time has been granted under Rule 7(b)(1) or Rule 27(c). The court reporter or transcriptionist shall certify to the clerk of the trial tribunal that the transcript has been so delivered and shall send a copy of such certification to the appellate court to which the appeal is taken. The appellant shall promptly notify the court reporter when the record on appeal has been filed. Once the court reporter, or person designated to prepare the transcript, has been notified by the appellant that the record on appeal has been filed with the appellate court to which the appeal has been taken, the court reporter must electronically file the transcript with that court using the docket number assigned by that court.

(3) Neutral Transcriptionist. The neutral person designated to prepare the transcript shall not be a relative or employee or attorney or counsel of any of the parties, or a relative or employee of such attorney or counsel, or be financially interested in the action unless the parties agree otherwise by stipulation.

Note that pursuant to Rule 7, there are different procedures for requesting or providing a transcript. In civil cases, within fourteen days after the entry of the notice of appeal, the appellant must arrange for a transcriptionist to prepare a transcript.[21] After wards, the appellant must inform the trial clerk of the transcript arrangements. The same procedure goes for criminal cases where the defendant appellant is not indigent.

In criminal cases where the defendant appellant is indigent, it is the duty of the trial court clerk to order a transcript after preparing an appellate entries form, serving the parties with the final order, and a statement naming the parties, their attorneys and how many transcripts were ordered.[22]

After the transcript is ordered, the transcriptionist has sixty days to complete the transcript. Motions to extend this time are routinely filed for cases with long trials or hearings. In criminal capital cases, the transcriptionist has 120 days. In expedited juvenile cases, the transcriptionist has thirty-five days. Transcriptionists are now required to include an electronic copy of the transcript.

---

21   *Page v. Canoutas*, 148 N.C. App. 406, 560 S.E.2d 886 (2002).
22   *See State v. Berryman, supra.*

CHAPTER SIX: STAY ON APPEAL

Rule 8(a) addresses stays pending appeal in civil cases, while Rule 8(b) applies to criminal cases only. A stay may be requested when there is reason to believe that if the trial court's order is carried out, there may be irreparable harm should the appellate court hold otherwise. If the trial court refuses to stay the execution or enforcement of the order, counsel may apply to the Court of Appeals for a Writ of Supersedeas under Rule 23[23], which is discussed later in this manual. Remember that any trial court order that is "entered" is effective unless a stay is entered. If the appellant does not move to stay the execution of the order, the directives in the order must be carried out.[24]

The Court of Appeals has held that a pending appeal of an adjudication of abuse and neglect is made moot by a subsequent termination of parental rights if the TPR order was based on "independent grounds."[25]

RULE 8: Stay Pending Appeal.

(a) Stay in Civil Cases. When appeal is taken in a civil action from a judgment, order, or other determination of a trial court, stay of execution or enforcement thereof pending disposition of the appeal must ordinarily first be sought by the deposit of security with the clerk of the superior court in those cases for which provision is made by law for the entry of stays upon deposit of adequate security, or by application to the trial court for a stay order in all other cases. After a stay order or entry has been denied or vacated by a trial court, an appellant may apply to the appropriate appellate court for a temporary stay and a writ of supersedeas in accordance with Rule 23. In any appeal which is

---

23   *See In re Burgess*, 57 N.C. App. 268, 291 S.E.2d 323 (1982).
24   *Id.*
25   *See In re N.B.*, 163 N.C. App. 182, 592 S.E.2d 597 (2004), *aff'd*, 359 N.C. 627, 614 S.E.2d 532 (2005) (trial judge specifically noted that TPR order was based on some evidence presented at adjudication hearing but not on the previous adjudication of abuse and neglect itself)

allowed by law to be taken from an agency to the appellate division, application for the temporary stay and writ of supersedeas may be made to the appellate court in the first instance. Application for the temporary stay and writ of supersedeas may similarly be made to the appellate court in the first instance when extraordinary circumstances make it impracticable to obtain a stay by deposit of security or by application to the trial court for a stay order.

(b) Stay in Criminal Cases. When a defendant has given notice of appeal, those portions of criminal sentences which impose fines or costs are automatically stayed pursuant to the provisions of N.C.G.S. § 15A-1451. Stays of imprisonment or of the execution of death sentences must be pursued under N.C.G.S. § 15A-536 or Rule 23.

CHAPTER SEVEN: THE RECORD ON APPEAL

Arguably the most important document filed at the appellate level, the Record on Appeal, includes everything necessary for an understanding of the case. Attorneys may not refer to anything outside of what is included in the Record on Appeal.[26] Rule 9 describes the contents of the record on appeal. Although this rule is more important from the appellant's perspective, the appellee should still be aware of what the record should contain. Rule 9(a) concerns the function of the record on appeal. Specifically, it limits appellate review to the transcript and contents of the record on appeal. If responding to a brief that cites to items not contained in the record, counsel should file a motion to dismiss all or part of the argument that cites to items outside the record.[27]

The Court made two drastic changes to this Rule. There is now no requirement to include assignments of error in the Record on Appeal. The appellant simply needs to present proposed issues, thus, eliminating appellants' need to list a multitude of possible errors regarding findings of fact or conclusions of law, etc., that may be discussed in the brief.

The other change is the supplemental filing of additional documents. Previously, appellees' documents could only come in by responding to the proposed record on appeal or moving the court to add documents to the record on appeal. Now, you can simply file a supplement to the record on appeal without first obtaining the court's permission. However, beware of putting too much in the record.[28]

---

26   *State v. Fair*, 354 N.C. 131, 166-67, 557 S.E.2d 500, 525 (2001), *cert. denied*, 535 U.S. 1114, 122 S. Ct. 2332, 153 L. Ed. 2d 162 (2002).

27   *See Duke Univ. v. Bishop*, 131 N.C. App. 545, 507 S.E.2d 904 (1998) (appellants attempted to include memoranda of law and a letter to the trial court as an appendix to their brief despite trial court order prohibiting the inclusion of those documents in the record on appeal).

28   *See In re J.J.* (unpublished, available at 2009 WL 2930640) (where Court of Appeals admonished all counsel for filing a record 770 pages long)

RULE 9: The Record on Appeal.

(a) Function; Composition of record. In appeals from the trial division of the General Court of Justice, review is solely upon the record on appeal, the verbatim transcript of proceedings, if one is designated, constituted in accordance with this Rule 9, and any items filed with the record on appeal pursuant to Rule 9(c) and 9(d). Parties may cite any of these items in their briefs and arguments before the appellate courts.

(1) Composition of the record in civil actions and special proceedings. The record on appeal in civil actions and special proceedings shall contain:

a. an index of the contents of the record, which shall appear as the first page thereof;

b. a statement identifying the judge from whose judgment or order appeal is taken, the session at which the judgment or order was rendered, or if rendered out of session, the time and place of rendition, and the party appealing;

c. a copy of the summons with return, or of other papers showing jurisdiction of the trial court over person or property, or a statement showing same;

d. copies of the pleadings, and of any pre-trial order on which the case or any part thereof was tried;

e. so much of the evidence, set out in the form provided in Rule 9(c)(1), as is necessary for an understanding of all errors assigned, or a statement specifying that the verbatim transcript of proceedings is being filed with the record pursuant to Rule 9(c)(2), or designating portions of the transcript to be so filed;

f. where error is assigned to the giving or omission of instructions to the jury, a transcript of the entire charge given;

g. copies of the issues submitted and the verdict, or of the trial court's findings of fact and conclusions of law;

h. a copy of the judgment, order, or other determination from which appeal is taken;

i. a copy of the notice of appeal, of all orders establishing time limits relative to the perfecting of the appeal, of any order finding a party to the appeal to be a civil pauper, and of any agreement, notice of approval, or order settling the record on appeal and settling the verbatim transcript of proceedings if one is filed pursuant to Rule 9(c)(2) and (3);

j. copies of all other papers filed and statements of all other proceedings had in the trial court which are necessary to an understanding of all errors assigned unless they appear in the verbatim transcript of proceedings which is being filed with the record pursuant to Rule 9(c)(2);

k. assignments of error set out in the manner provided in Rule 10; and

l. a statement, where appropriate, that the record of proceedings was made with an electronic recording device.

(2) Composition of the record in appeals from superior court review of administrative boards and agencies. The record on appeal in cases of appeal from judgments of the superior court rendered upon review of the proceedings of administrative boards or agencies, other than those specified in Rule 18(a), shall contain:

a. an index of the contents of the record, which shall appear as the first page thereof;

b. a statement identifying the judge from whose judgment or order appeal is taken, the session at which the judgment or order was rendered, or if rendered out of session, the time and place of rendition, and the party appealing;

c. a copy of the summons, notice of hearing or other papers showing jurisdiction of the board or agency over the persons or property sought to be bound in the proceeding, or a statement showing same;

d. copies of all petitions and other pleadings filed in the superior court;

e. copies of all items properly before the superior court as are necessary for an understanding of all errors assigned;

f. a copy of any findings of fact and conclusions of law and of the judgment, order, or other determination of the superior court from which appeal is taken;

g. a copy of the notice of appeal from the superior court, of all orders establishing time limits relative to the perfecting of the appeal, of any order finding a party to the appeal to be a civil pauper, and of any agreement, notice of approval, or order settling the record on appeal and settling the verbatim transcript of proceedings, if one is filed pursuant to Rule 9(c)(2) and (3); and

h. assignments of error to the actions of the superior court, set out in the manner provided in Rule 10.

(3) Composition of the record in criminal actions.
The record on appeal in criminal actions shall contain:

a. an index of the contents of the record, which shall appear as the first page thereof;

b. a statement identifying the judge from whose judgment or order appeal is taken, the session at which the judgment or order was rendered, or if rendered out of session, the time and place of rendition, and the party appealing;

c. copies of all warrants, informations, presentments, and indictments upon which the case has been tried in any court;

d. copies of docket entries or a statement showing all arraignments and pleas;

e. so much of the evidence, set out in the form provided in Rule 9(c)(1), as is necessary for an understanding of all errors assigned, or a statement that the entire verbatim transcript of the proceedings is being filed with the record pursuant to Rule 9(c)(2), or designating portions of the transcript to be so filed;

f. where error is assigned to the giving or omission of instructions to the jury, a transcript of the entire charge given;

g. copies of the verdict and of the judgment, order, or other determination from which appeal is taken; and in capitally tried cases, a copy of the jury verdict sheet for sentencing, showing the aggravating and mitigating circumstances submitted and found or not found;

h. a copy of the notice of appeal or an appropriate entry or statement showing appeal taken orally; of all orders establishing time limits relative to the perfecting of the appeal; of any order finding defendant indigent for the purposes of the appeal and assigning counsel; and of any agreement, notice of approval, or order settling the record on appeal and settling the verbatim transcript of proceedings, if one is to be filed pursuant to Rule 9(c)(2);

i. copies of all other papers filed and statements of all other proceedings had in the trial courts which are necessary for an understanding of all errors assigned, unless they appear in the verbatim transcript of proceedings which is being filed with the record pursuant to Rule 9(c)(2);

j. assignments of error set out in the manner provided in Rule 10;

k. a statement, where appropriate, that the record of proceedings was made with an electronic recording device; and

l. a statement, where appropriate, that a supplement compiled pursuant to Rule 11(c) is filed with the record on appeal.

(4) Exclusion of Social Security Numbers from Record on Appeal. Social security numbers shall be deleted or redacted from any document before including the document in the record on appeal.

The appellate courts are very strict about the formatting of the record on appeal[29]. Below in Rule 9(b), there are rules regarding the order of items in the record on appeal. In addition, Rule 9(b) provides for amendments to the Record on Appeal after it has been filed with the clerk at the appellate court.[30]

(b) Form of record; Amendments. The record on appeal shall be in the format prescribed by Rule 26(g) and the appendixes to these rules.

(1) Order of arrangement. The items constituting the record on appeal should be arranged, so far as practicable, in the order in which they occurred or were filed in the trial tribunal.

(2) Inclusion of unnecessary matter; Penalty. It shall be the duty of counsel for all parties to an appeal to avoid including in the record on appeal matter not necessary for an understanding of the errors assigned, such as social security numbers referred to in Rule 9(a)(4). The cost of including such matter may be charged as costs to the party or counsel who caused or permitted its inclusion.

(3) Filing dates and signatures on papers. Every pleading, motion, affidavit, or other paper included in the record on appeal shall show the date on which it was filed and, if verified, the date of verification and the person who verified. Every judgment, order, or other determination shall show the date on which it was entered. The typed or printed name of the person signing a paper shall be entered immediately below the signature.

(4) Pagination; Counsel identified. The pages of the record on appeal shall be numbered consecutively, be referred to as "record pages" and be cited as "(R p. _____)." Pages of the verbatim transcript of proceedings filed under Rule 9(c)(2) shall be referred to as "transcript pages" and cited as "(T p. _____)." At the end of the record on appeal shall appear the names, office addresses, and telephone numbers of counsel of record for all parties to the appeal.

---

29   *Crowell Constructors v. State ex rel. Cobey*, 328 N.C. 563, 402 S.E.2d 407 (1991).
30   *See State v. Petersilie*, 334 N.C. 169, 432 S.E.2d 832 (1993).

(5) Additions and amendments to record on appeal. On motion of any party or on its own initiative, the appellate court may order additional portions of a trial court record or transcript sent up and added to the record on appeal. On motion of any party the appellate court may order any portion of the record on appeal or transcript amended to correct error shown as to form or content. Prior to the filing of the record on appeal in the appellate court, such motions may be made by any party to the trial tribunal.

(6) Appeals from Termination of Parental Rights and Juvenile Matters. The record on appeal shall comply with the provisions to protect the confidentiality of juveniles by redacting the juvenile's name and other identifying information as set out in Rule 3(b) from any documents included in the record on appeal.

(c) Presentation of testimonial evidence and other proceedings. Testimonial evidence, voir dire, and other trial proceedings necessary to be presented for review by the appellate court may be included either in the record on appeal in the form specified in Rule 9(c)(1) or by designating the verbatim transcript of proceedings of the trial tribunal as provided in Rule 9(c)(2) and (c)(3). Where error is assigned to the giving or omission of instructions to the jury, a transcript of the entire charge given shall be included in the record on appeal. Verbatim transcripts in an appeal of a termination of parental rights or a juvenile matter, as identified by Rule 3(b), shall be submitted to the appellate court in a signed, sealed envelope or other appropriate container on which is noted a case caption that complies with the confidentiality provisions of Rule 3(b), including the District Court case number. The transcript shall be available to the public only with permission from the appellate court.

(1) When testimonial evidence narrated -- How set out in record. Where error is assigned with respect to the admission or exclusion of evidence, the question and answer form shall be utilized in setting out the pertinent questions and answers. Other testimonial evidence required to be included in the record on appeal by Rule 9(a) shall be set out in narrative form except where such form might not fairly reflect the true sense of the evidence received, in which case it may be set out in question and answer form. Counsel are expected to seek that form or combination of forms best calculated under the circumstances to present the true sense of the required testimonial evidence concisely and at a minimum of expense to the litigants. To this end, counsel may object to particular narration that it does not accurately reflect the true sense of testimony received; or to particular question and answer portions that the testimony

might with no substantial loss in accuracy be summarized in narrative form at substantially less expense. When a judge or referee is required to settle the record on appeal under Rule 11(c) and there is dispute as to the form, he shall settle the form in the course of his general settlement of the record on appeal.

(2) Designation that verbatim transcript of proceedings in trial tribunal will be used. Appellant may designate in the record on appeal that the testimonial evidence will be presented in the verbatim transcript of the evidence in the trial tribunal in lieu of narrating the evidence as permitted by Rule 9(c)(1). Appellant may also designate that the verbatim transcript will be used to present voir dire or other trial proceedings where those proceedings are the basis for one or more assignments of error and where a verbatim transcript of those proceedings has been made. Any such designation shall refer to the page numbers of the transcript being designated. Appellant need not designate all of the verbatim transcript which has been made, provided that when the verbatim transcript is designated to show the testimonial evidence, so much of the testimonial evidence must be designated as is necessary for an understanding of all errors assigned. When appellant has narrated the evidence and trial proceedings under Rule 9(c)(1), the appellee may designate the verbatim transcript as a proposed alternative record on appeal.

(3) Verbatim transcript of proceedings -- Settlement, filing, copies, briefs. Whenever a verbatim transcript is designated to be used pursuant to Rule 9(c) (2):

a. it shall be settled, together with the record on appeal, according to the procedures established by Rule 11;

b. appellant shall cause the settled, verbatim transcript to be filed, contemporaneously with the record on appeal, with the clerk of the appellate court in which the appeal is docketed;

c. in criminal appeals, the district attorney, upon settlement of the record on appeal, shall forward one copy of the settled transcript to the Attorney General of North Carolina; and

d. the briefs of the parties must comport with the requirements of Rule 28 regarding complete statement of the facts of the case and regarding appendixes to the briefs.

(4) Presentation of discovery materials. Discovery materials offered into evidence at trial shall be brought forward, if relevant, as other evidence. In all instances where discovery materials are considered by the trial tribunal, other

than as evidence offered at trial, the following procedures for presenting those materials to the appellate court shall be used: Depositions shall be treated as testimonial evidence and shall be presented by narration or by transcript of the deposition in the manner prescribed by this Rule 9(c). Other discovery materials, including interrogatories and answers, requests for admission, responses to requests, motions to produce, and the like, pertinent to questions raised on appeal, may be set out in the record on appeal or may be sent up as documentary exhibits in accordance with Rule 9(d)(2).

(5) Electronic Recordings. When a narrative or transcript has been prepared from an electronic recording, the parties shall not file a copy of the electronic recording with the appellate division except at the direction or with the approval of the appellate court.

(d) Models, diagrams, and exhibits of material.

(1) Exhibits. Maps, plats, diagrams and other documentary exhibits filed as portions of or attachments to items required to be included in the record on appeal shall be included as part of such items in the record on appeal. Where such exhibits are not necessary to an understanding of the errors assigned, they may by agreement of counsel or by order of the trial court upon motion be excluded from the record on appeal. Social security numbers shall be deleted or redacted from exhibits prior to filing the exhibits in the appellate court.

(2) Transmitting exhibits. Three legible copies of each documentary exhibit offered in evidence and required for understanding of errors assigned shall be filed in the appellate court; the original documentary exhibit need not be filed with the appellate court. When an original non-documentary exhibit has been settled as a necessary part of the record on appeal, any party may within 10 days after settlement of the record on appeal in writing request the clerk of superior court to transmit the exhibit directly to the clerk of the appellate court. The clerk shall thereupon promptly identify and transmit the exhibit as directed by the party. Upon receipt of the exhibit, the clerk of the appellate court shall make prompt written acknowledgment thereof to the transmitting clerk and the exhibit shall be included as part of the records in the appellate court. Portions of the record on appeal in either appellate court which are not suitable for reproduction may be designated by the Clerk of the Supreme Court to be exhibits. Counsel may then be required to submit three additional copies of those designated materials.

(3) Removal of exhibits from appellate court. All models, diagrams, and exhibits of material placed in the custody of the Clerk of the appellate court must be taken away by the parties within 90 days after the mandate of the Court has issued or the case has otherwise been closed by withdrawal, dismissal, or other order of the Court, unless notified otherwise by the Clerk. When this is not done, the Clerk shall notify counsel to remove the articles forthwith; and if they are not removed within a reasonable time after such notice, the Clerk shall destroy them, or make such other disposition of them as to the Clerk may seem best.

Although some attorneys move to amend the record on appeal in their briefs, the better practice is to make a motion to amend as soon as you know the motion is needed. Rule 9(c), as it applies to juvenile cases, requires that verbatim transcripts from termination of parental rights trial or other juvenile matters be submitted to the appellate court "in a signed, sealed envelope or other appropriate container on which is noted a case caption that complies with confidentiality provisions." The transcript cannot be made available to the public without permission from the appellate court. In addition, there is the possibility of using a narration of the trial proceedings where a verbatim transcript is not available.[31] Juvenile cases often are recorded, and the recording equipment assigned to districts may be unreliable. If the tape of the proceedings cannot be transcribed for any reason, counsel's goal should be to reproduce as closely as possible the dialogue between counsel and witnesses in question-and-answer format.

While the Rules appear to permit litigants to use narration in lieu of verbatim transcripts even if a transcript is available, N.C. Gen. Stat. § 7B-806 mandates that in juvenile cases, "[all] adjudicatory and dispositional hearings be recorded by stenographic notes or by electronic or mechanical means." No matter how the trial court testimony is reproduced, the appellant must designate the form of the transcript (i.e. narration or verbatim). Appellants generally include an explanation of why a narrative was used in the designation.[32] The designation may refer to only certain portions of the transcript, but if the appellant chooses only specific pages of the transcript, the appellant must specifically identify those pages. If the verbatim transcript is not particularly long, counsel should insist that the entire transcript be included in the record on appeal. However, if the transcript is long, and the appellant designates only certain portions of

---

31   *See State v. Quick*, 179 N.C. App. 647, 651, 634 S.E.2d 915, 918 (2006).

32   *See In re Bradshaw*, 160 N.C. App. 677, 587 S.E.2d 83 (2003) (finding no prejudice where one day of testimony in a TPR hearing went unrecorded, and the appellant father made no attempt to reconstruct the missing testimony).

the transcript for the record on appeal, counsel must be sure those portions include the pages upon which he or she may need to rely.

Rules 9(c)(3)-(5) sets out additional requirements for the record on appeal. Rule 9(c)(3) requires the verbatim transcript to be settled along with the record on appeal, and it mandates that the appellant file a copy of the verbatim transcript at the same time the party files the record on appeal.[33] The rule also refers to Rule 28 in regards to the statement of the facts and appendices in briefs, which is discussed in more detail under Rule 28 of this manual. Rule 9(c)(4) involves the proper presentation of discovery materials in the record on appeal. "Testimonial" forms of discovery materials are treated pursuant to Rule 9(c), while other materials can be treated similarly or as an exhibit under Rule 9(d), below. Rule 9(c)(5) states that it is not necessary to file a copy of the recording (i.e. tape) in the record on appeal if the transcript was prepared from an "electronic recording." Rules 9(d)(1)-(3) address treatment of exhibits in the record on appeal, including trial exhibits —if any— and other documents "necessary to an understanding of the errors assigned." [34]Counsel must remember to redact any identifying information in these exhibits in juvenile cases.

RULE 10: Preservation of Issues At Trial; Proposed Issues On Appeal.

Since the court did away with assignments of error, it necessarily omitted much of the former Rule 10. However, you still must properly preserved issues for appellate review.[35] Rule 10 explains how the appellate court's review is restricted. The appellate court does not take the entire trial court file and sort through it find possible errors. Rule 10(a) specifies the need for preserving issues. Rule 10(b) discusses how questions may be preserved for appellate review. Rules 10(c) and (d) explain the format of assignments of error and cross-assignments of error.

Rule 10(a) sets out the scope of appellate review and limits it to the issues contained in the record on appeal. These issues may be based upon (1) whether the judgment is properly supported by findings of fact and conclusions of law and (2) whether the trial court had proper subject matter jurisdiction.[36]

---

33   *See Joker Club, L.L.C. v. Hardin*, 183 N.C. App. 92, 643 S.E.2d 626 (2007).

34   *Id.*

35   *Pfeifer v. Jones & Laughlin Steel Corp.*, 678 F.2d 453, 457 n.1 (3d Cir. 1982), *vacated and remanded on other grounds*, 462 U.S. 523, 103 S. Ct. 2541, 76 L. Ed. 2d 768 (1983).

36   *See In re P.M.*, 169 N.C. App. 423, 424, 610 S.E.2d 403, 405 (2005) (since appellant mother specifically assigned error to only three of the trial court's findings of fact, the remaining findings of fact were binding on appeal). *See also Wade v. Wade*, 72 N.C. App. 372, 375, 325 S.E.2d 260, 266 , *disc. rev. denied*, 313 N.C. 612, 330 S.E.2d 616 (1985) (single assignment of error generally challenging

Rule 10(b) requires appellants to properly preserve questions for appellate review. Under this section, the appellant must present to the trial court a timely request, objection or motion, stating the specific grounds for the ruling that the party desired the court to make (if the specific grounds are not apparent from the context).[37]

Rule 10(c) now discusses stating issues for review instead of assignments of error. All issues must be numbered, stated "without argument" and "state plainly, concisely and without argumentation the legal basis upon which error is assigned." Rule 10(c) allows appellants to argue outside of the issues presented on appeal in the record.

Rule 10(d) discusses cross-assignments of error. It is an excellent tool for the appellee. This rule allows an appellee to discuss issues under certain conditions without taking a cross-appeal.[38] By allowing appellee proposed issues, the rule permits the appellee to remedy the trial court's errors by showing alternative bases in law that would support the trial court's judgments.[39] Appellees asserting proposed issues should support them in the record on appeal by including relevant documents and/or testimony.

(a) Preserving Issues During Trial Proceedings.

(1) General. In order to preserve an issue for appellate review, a party must have presented to the trial court a timely request, objection, or motion, stating the specific grounds for the ruling the party desired the court to make if the specific grounds were not apparent from the context. It is also necessary for the complaining party to obtain a ruling upon the party's request, objection, or motion. Any such issue that was properly preserved for review by action of counsel taken during the course of proceedings in the trial tribunal by objection noted or which by rule or law was deemed preserved or taken without any such action, including, but not limited to, whether the judgment is supported by the verdict or by the findings of fact and conclusions of law, whether the

---

the sufficiency of evidence to support numerous findings of fact held "broadside and ineffective" under Rule 10).

37 *See In re L.L.*, 172 N.C. App. 689, 695, 616 S.E.2d 392, 396 (2005) (DSS could not raise, on appeal, the question of whether the judge improperly retained jurisdiction over the case, because it did not raise the issue before the trial court); *In re E.T.S.*, 175 N.C. App. 32, 38-39, 623 S.E.2d 300, 304 (2005) (court refused to review the admission of neglect and dependency orders when the appellant mother did not contest those orders in the TPR proceeding).

38 *See generally Speagle v. Seitz*, 354 N.C. 525, 557 S.E.2d 83 (2001).

39 *State v. Wise*, 326 N.C. 421, 428, 390 S.E.2d 142, 146 (1990).

court had jurisdiction over the subject matter, and whether a criminal charge is sufficient in law, may be made the basis of an issue presented on appeal.

(2) Jury Instructions. A party may not make any portion of the jury charge or omission therefrom the basis of an issue presented on appeal unless the party objects thereto before the jury retires to consider its verdict, stating distinctly that to which objection is made and the grounds of the objection; provided that opportunity was given to the party to make the objection out of the hearing of the jury, and, on request of any party, out of the presence of the jury.

(3) Sufficiency of the Evidence. In a criminal case, a defendant may not make insufficiency of the evidence to prove the crime charged the basis of an issue presented on appeal unless a motion to dismiss the action, or for judgment as in case of nonsuit, is made at trial. If a defendant makes such a motion after the State has presented all its evidence and has rested its case and that motion is denied and the defendant then introduces evidence, defendant's motion for dismissal or judgment in case of nonsuit made at the close of State's evidence is waived. Such a waiver precludes the defendant from urging the denial of such motion as a ground for appeal.

A defendant may make a motion to dismiss the action, or for judgment as in case of nonsuit, at the conclusion of all the evidence, irrespective of whether defendant made an earlier such motion. If the motion at the close of all the evidence is denied, the defendant may urge as ground for appeal the denial of the motion made at the conclusion of all the evidence. However, if a defendant fails to move to dismiss the action, or for judgment as in case of nonsuit, at the close of all the evidence, defendant may not challenge on appeal the sufficiency of the evidence to prove the crime charged.

If a defendant's motion to dismiss the action, or for judgment as in case of nonsuit, is allowed, or shall be sustained on appeal, it shall have the force and effect of a verdict of "not guilty" as to such defendant.

(4) Plain Error. In criminal cases, an issue that was not preserved by objection noted at trial and that is not deemed preserved by rule or law without any such action nevertheless may be made the basis of an issue presented on appeal when the judicial action questioned is specifically and distinctly contended to amount to plain error.

(b) Appellant's Proposed Issues on Appeal. Proposed issues that the appellant intends to present on appeal shall be stated without argument at the conclusion of the record on appeal in a numbered list. Proposed issues on appeal are to facilitate the preparation of the record on appeal and shall not limit the scope of the issues presented on appeal in an appellant's brief.

(c) Appellee's Proposed Issues on Appeal as to an Alternative Basis in Law. Without taking an appeal, an appellee may list proposed issues on appeal in the record on appeal based on any action or omission of the trial court that was properly preserved for appellate review and that deprived the appellee of an alternative basis in law for supporting the judgment, order, or other determination from which appeal has been taken. An appellee's list of proposed issues on appeal shall not preclude an appellee from presenting arguments on other issues in its brief.

Portions of the record or transcript of proceedings necessary to an understanding of such proposed issues on appeal as to an alternative basis in law may be included in the record on appeal by agreement of the parties under Rule 11(a), may be included by the appellee in a proposed alternative record on appeal under Rule 11(b), or may be designated for inclusion in the verbatim transcript of proceedings, if one is filed under Rule 9(c)(2).

RULE 11: Settling the Record on Appeal.

The appellant puts together a proposed record on appeal and serves it on the appellee(s). The appellee can object to items in the record or request amendments or additions to the record.[40] The appellee has thirty days to respond to the proposed record on appeal. If no response is received within that time, the proposed record on appeal constitutes the record on appeal. Should parties be unable to agree on what should or should not be included in the record, the appellee may file an alternate record on appeal. Rule 9(b)(6) requires that the record on appeal be redacted to protect the identity of any juveniles. As a matter of practice, counsel adding to the proposed record on appeal should redact the proposed additional documents before sending them to the opposing counsel for inclusion in the record.

(a) By Agreement. This rule applies to all cases except those subject to expedited schedules in Rule 3.1.

---

40   *Day v. Day*, 180 N.C. App. 685, 637 S.E.2d 906 (2006).

Within thirty-five days after the reporter or transcriptionist certifies delivery of the transcript, if such was ordered (seventy days in capitally tried cases), or thirty-five days after appellant files notice of appeal, whichever is later, the parties may by agreement entered in the record on appeal settle a proposed record on appeal prepared by any party in accordance with Rule 9 as the record on appeal.

(b) By Appellee's Approval of Appellant's Proposed Record on Appeal. If the record on appeal is not settled by agreement under Rule 11(a), the appellant shall, within the same times provided, serve upon all other parties a proposed record on appeal constituted in accordance with the provisions of Rule 9. Within thirty days (thirty-five days in capitally tried cases) after service of the proposed record on appeal upon an appellee, that appellee may serve upon all other parties a notice of approval of the proposed record on appeal, or objections, amendments, or a proposed alternative record on appeal in accordance with Rule 11(c). If all appellees within the times allowed them either serve notices of approval or fail to serve either notices of approval or objections, amendments, or proposed alternative records on appeal, appellant's proposed record on appeal thereupon constitutes the record on appeal.

(c) By Agreement, by Operation of Rule, or by Court Order After Appellee's Objection or Amendment. Within thirty days (thirty-five days in capitally tried cases) after service upon appellee of appellant's proposed record on appeal, that appellee may serve upon all other parties specific amendments or objections to the proposed record on appeal, or a proposed alternative record on appeal. Amendments or objections to the proposed record on appeal shall be set out in a separate paper and shall specify any item(s) for which an objection is based on the contention that the item was not filed, served, submitted for consideration, admitted, or made the subject of an offer of proof, or that the content of a statement or narration is factually inaccurate. An appellant who objects to an appellee's response to the proposed record on appeal shall make the same specification in its request for judicial settlement. The formatting of the proposed record on appeal and the order in which items appear in it are the responsibility of the appellant.

If any appellee timely serves amendments, objections, or a proposed alternative record on appeal, the record on appeal shall consist of each item that is either among those items required by Rule 9(a) to be in the record on appeal or that is requested by any party to the appeal and agreed upon for inclusion by all other parties to the appeal. If a party requests that an item be included in the record on appeal but not all other parties to the appeal agree to its inclusion, then that item shall not be included in the printed record on appeal, but shall be filed by the appellant with the printed record on appeal in three copies of a volume captioned "Rule 11(c) Supplement to the Printed Record on Appeal," along with any verbatim transcripts, narrations of proceedings, documentary exhibits, and other items that are filed pursuant to Rule 9(c) or 9(d); provided that any item not filed, served, submitted for consideration, or admitted, or for which no offer of proof was tendered, shall not be included. Subject to the additional requirements of Rule 28(d), items in the Rule 11(c) supplement may be cited and used by the parties as would items in the printed record on appeal.

If a party does not agree to the wording of a statement or narration required or permitted by these rules, there shall be no judicial settlement to resolve the dispute unless the objection is based on a contention that the statement or narration concerns an item that was not filed, served, submitted for consideration, admitted, or tendered in an offer of proof, or that a statement or narration is factually inaccurate. Instead, the objecting party is permitted to have inserted in the settled record on appeal a concise counter-statement. Parties are strongly encouraged to reach agreement on the wording of statements in records on appeal. Judicial settlement is not appropriate for disputes that concern only the formatting of a record on appeal or the order in which items appear in a record on appeal.

The Rule 11(c) supplement to the printed record on appeal shall contain an index of the contents of the supplement, which shall appear as the first page thereof. The Rule 11(c) supplement shall be paginated as required by Rule 9(b)(4) and the contents should be arranged, so far as practicable, in the order in which they occurred or were filed in the trial tribunal. If a party does not agree to the inclusion or specification of an exhibit or transcript in the printed record, the printed record shall include a statement that such items are separately filed along with the supplement.

If any party to the appeal contends that materials proposed for inclusion in the record or for filing therewith pursuant to Rule 9(c) or 9(d) were not filed, served, submitted for consideration, admitted, or made the subject of an offer of proof, or that a statement or narration permitted by these rules is not factually accurate, then that party, within ten days after expiration of the time within which the appellee last served with the appellant's proposed record on appeal might have served amendments, objections, or a proposed alternative record on appeal, may in writing request that the judge from whose judgment, order, or other determination appeal was taken settle the record on appeal. A copy of the request, endorsed with a certificate showing service on the judge, shall be filed forthwith in the office of the clerk of the superior court and served upon all other parties. Each party shall promptly provide to the judge a reference copy of the record items, amendments, or objections served by that party in the case.

The functions of the judge in the settlement of the record on appeal are to determine whether a statement permitted by these rules is not factually accurate, to settle narrations of proceedings under Rule 9(c)(1), and to determine whether the record accurately reflects material filed, served, submitted for consideration, admitted, or made the subject of an offer of proof, but not to decide whether material desired in the record by either party is relevant to the issues on appeal, non-duplicative, or otherwise suited for inclusion in the record on appeal.

The judge shall send written notice to counsel for all parties setting a place and a time for a hearing to settle the record on appeal. The hearing shall be held not later than fifteen days after service of the request for hearing upon the judge. The judge shall settle the record on appeal by order entered not more than twenty days after service of the request for hearing upon the judge. If requested, the judge shall return the record items submitted for reference during the judicial settlement process with the order settling the record on appeal.

If any appellee timely serves amendments, objections, or a proposed alternative record on appeal, and no judicial settlement of the record is timely sought, the record is deemed settled as of the expiration of the ten day period within which any party could have requested judicial settlement of the record on appeal under this Rule 11(c).

Provided that, nothing herein shall prevent settlement of the record on appeal by agreement of the parties at any time within the times herein limited for settling the record by judicial order.

(d) Multiple Appellants; Single Record on Appeal. When there are multiple appellants (two or more), whether proceeding separately or jointly, as parties aligned in interest, or as cross-appellants, there shall nevertheless be but one record on appeal. The proposed issues on appeal of the several appellants shall be set out separately in the single record on appeal and attributed to the several appellants by any clear means of reference. In the event multiple appellants cannot agree to the procedure for constituting a proposed record on appeal, the judge from whose judgment, order, or other determination the appeals are taken shall, on motion of any appellant with notice to all other appellants, enter an order settling the procedure, including the allocation of costs.

(e) Extensions of Time. The times provided in this rule for taking any action may be extended in accordance with the provisions of Rule 27(c).

RULE 12: Filing the Record.

Rule 12 is very clear on the time limits for serving the Record on Appeal. It addresses the filing of the record on appeal and provides that, when the appellant is indigent pursuant to N.C. Gen. Stat. § 1-288 or 7A-450, the appellate clerk will docket the appeal without payment. The appellate clerk then notifies the parties to the appeal of the date on which the appeal was docketed. Rule 12 allows the appellant in civil cases 15 days from the time the record is settled to file the record on appeal. However, Rule 3A applies to GAL cases and allows only five days. Rule 3A also requires the appellant to file three "legible" copies of the record on appeal, whereas Rule 12 requires the appellant to file only one copy.

(a) Time for Filing Record on Appeal. Within fifteen days after the record on appeal has been settled by any of the procedures provided in Rule 11 or Rule 18, the appellant shall file the record on appeal with the clerk of the court to which appeal is taken.

(b) Docketing the Appeal. At the time of filing the record on appeal, the appellant shall pay to the clerk the docket fee fixed pursuant to N.C.G.S. § 7A-20(b), and the clerk shall thereupon enter the appeal upon the docket of the appellate court. If an appellant is authorized to appeal in forma pauperis as provided in N.C.G.S. §§ 1-288 or 7A-450 et seq., the clerk shall docket the appeal upon timely filing of the record on appeal. An appeal is docketed under the title given to the action in the trial division, with the appellant identified as such. The clerk shall forthwith give notice to all parties of the date on which the appeal was docketed in the appellate court.

(c) Copies of Record on Appeal. The appellant shall file one copy of the record on appeal, three copies of each exhibit designated pursuant to Rule 9(d), three copies of any supplement to the record on appeal submitted pursuant to Rule 11(c) or Rule 18(d)(3) and shall cause the transcript to be filed electronically pursuant to Rule 7. The clerk will reproduce and distribute copies as directed by the court, billing the parties pursuant to these rules.

RULE THIRTEEN: Filing and Service of Briefs.

The dates that the briefs are due are based on the date the Record on Appeal was filed. As you see in Rule 13, the appellant has 30 days after the Record on Appeal has been filed to file and serve its brief. The appellee has 30 days from receipt of the appellant's brief to file its brief. The three extra days for mailing does not calculate into the 30-day timeline. Failure to follow these time limits can result in the dismissal of the action or striking the untimely brief.[41]

(a) Time for Filing and Service of Briefs.

(1) Cases Other Than Death Penalty Cases. Within thirty days after the clerk of the appellate court has mailed the printed record to the parties, the appellant shall file a brief in the office of the clerk of the appellate court and serve copies thereof upon all other parties separately represented. The mailing of the printed record is not service for purposes of Rule 27(b); therefore, the provision of that rule allowing an additional three days after service by mail does not extend the period for the filing of an appellant's brief. Within thirty days after appellant's brief has been served on an appellee, the appellee shall similarly file and serve copies of a brief. If permitted by Rule 28(h), the appellant may serve and file a reply brief as provided in that rule.

(2) Death Penalty Cases. Within sixty days after the clerk of the Supreme Court has mailed the printed record to the parties, the appellant in a criminal appeal which includes a sentence of death shall file a brief in the office of the clerk and serve copies thereof upon all other parties separately represented. The mailing of the printed record is not service for purposes of Rule 27(b); therefore, the provision of that rule allowing an additional three days after service by mail does not extend the period for the filing of an appellant's brief. Within sixty days after appellant's brief has been served, the appellee shall similarly file and

---

41   *Holland, supra.*

serve copies of a brief. If permitted by Rule 28(h), the appellant may serve and file a reply brief as provided in that rule, except that reply briefs filed pursuant to Rule 28(h)(2) or (h)(3) shall be filed and served within twenty-one days after service of the appellee's brief.

(b) Copies Reproduced by Clerk. A party need file but a single copy of a brief. At the time of filing the party may be required to pay to the clerk of the appellate court a deposit fixed by the clerk to cover the cost of reproducing copies of the brief. The clerk will reproduce and distribute copies of briefs as directed by the court.

(c) Consequence of Failure to File and Serve Briefs. If an appellant fails to file and serve a brief within the time allowed, the appeal may be dismissed on motion of an appellee or on the court's own initiative. If an appellee fails to file and serve its brief within the time allowed, the appellee may not be heard in oral argument except by permission of the court.

An appellee may bring a motion to dismiss for failure to comply with the timing requirements of Rule 3.1, or the court may on its own initiative dismiss the appeal.[42] See Rule 28 for more in-depth rules on briefs.

---

42   *See Simmons v. Arriola*, 160 N.C. App. 671, 586 S.E.2d 809 (2003) (parent's appeal dismissed in custody proceeding where parent did not file brief within 30 days after the record on appeal was mailed and no extension was sought); *Holland v. Heavner*, 164 N.C. App. 218, 595 S.E.2d 224 (2004) (dismissal required where appellants did not file brief until 23 days after its due date).

CHAPTER EIGHT: BRIEFS

Rule 14 addresses appeals of right to the N.C. Supreme Court pursuant to N.C. Gen. Stat. § 7A-30. Under section 7A-30, a party to an appeal in the N.C. Court of Appeals has the right to appeal in cases that (1) directly involve "a substantial question arising under the Constitution of the United States or this State" or (2) "in which there is a dissent." Parties can only appeal a very limited number of cases to the Supreme Court without going through the more involved and time-consuming discretionary review process, which makes Rule 14 extremely important.

Rule 14(a) describes the timing and procedure for filing and serving notice of appeal to the Supreme Court. The appellant receives 15 days from the Court of Appeals' "mandate," or opinion, to file and serve notice of appeal to the Supreme Court. However, if a party files a petition for rehearing with the Court of Appeals, this 15-day period is tolled. Any other party that appeals to the Supreme Court must file notice of appeal within 10 days from the date of the filing of the first notice of appeal.

Rule 14(a) also explains the more complicated matter of handling an appeal to the Supreme Court where only some of the issues may be appealed of right. If not all issues are "appealed of right," the appealing party must file both a petition for discretionary review under Rule 15(c) and notice of appeal under Rule 14(a).

Rule 14(b) describes the required content in the notice of appeal. If the appeal is based on a dissent in the Court of Appeals, Rule 14(b)(1) applies. The appellant must include the: (1) name of the party taking the appeal, (2) Court of Appeals docket number and case caption, (3) statement that the appeal is being taken pursuant to N.C. Gen. Stat. § 7A-30 and (4) issues which are the bases for the dissenting opinion and which of those issues are being appealed.

If the appeal is based on a constitutional question, Rule 14(b)(2) applies. The requirements are the same as Rule 14(b)(1), except that in lieu of (4) above, the notice must contain a statement of the issues that form the basis for the appeal and the specific constitutional provisions upon which those issues are based. Also, the appellant must specifically explain how the appellant's rights were violated and state affirmatively that the constitutional issue was raised at either the trial court or Court of Appeals.

Rule (14)(c)(1) provides that the record on appeal in the Supreme Court is the same record on appeal that was used in the Court of Appeals. If the Supreme Court finds the record on appeal to be unsatisfactory, the Court can tweak the record or even dismiss the appeal.

If the appellant failed to raise the constitutional question to the trial court or Court of Appeals, and the issue could have been raised in either forum, the appellee should move to dismiss the Supreme Court appeal. An appellant cannot remedy the failure to raise a constitutional question by first raising the question to the Supreme Court. *See State v. Mitchell,* 276 N.C. 404, 410, 172 S.E.2d 527, 531 (1970) (holding that a constitutional right may be forfeited in criminal as well as civil cases by the failure to make timely assertion of the right before a tribunal having jurisdiction to determine it).

Under Rule 14(c)(2), court clerks handle the process for docketing the case in the Supreme Court, including reproduction and distribution of the record on appeal. There is little or no attorney involvement.

Rule 14(d)(1) sets out the guidelines for briefing cases in the Supreme Court. The appellant receives 30 days to file a new brief in the Court after notice of appeal is filed. The rule also describes the requirements for a Supreme Court brief and refers to Rule 28, which is discussed below.

If Supreme Court review is based upon a constitutional question, or discretionary questions are raised in the notice of appeal, the appellant receives 30 days after the Supreme Court rules on the petition for discretionary review to submit its new brief to the Court. The appellee must file a response within 30 days from the date of service of the new brief. If a reply brief is permitted under Rule 28(h), the appellant will receive an additional 15 days from the date of service of the appellee's brief in which to file a reply brief.

Rule 14(d)(1) discusses the possibility of a deposit to cover the costs of reproducing the brief. Under N.C. Gen. Stat. § 7B-2000, all juveniles are presumed indigent. So, if you are filing an appeal on the child's behalf, you are exempt from this rule.

Rule 14(d)(2) sets out the possible penalties for failure to file or serve a brief within the time limits. This rule allows the Supreme Court to either (1) dismiss the appeal in its entirety or (2) refuse to hear oral argument.[43]

RULE 14. Appeals of Right from Court of Appeals to Supreme Court Under G.S. 7a-30

(a) Notice of Appeal; Filing and Service. Appeals of right from the Court of Appeals to the Supreme Court are taken by filing notices of appeal with the clerk of the Court of Appeals and with the clerk of the Supreme Court and serving notice of appeal upon all other parties within fifteen days after the mandate of the Court of Appeals has been issued to the trial tribunal. For cases which arise from the Industrial Commission, a copy of the notice of appeal shall be served on the Chair of the Industrial Commission. The running of the time for filing and serving a notice of appeal is tolled as to all parties by the filing by any party within such time of a petition for rehearing under Rule 31 of these rules, and the full time for appeal thereafter commences to run and is computed as to all parties from the date of entry by the Court of Appeals of an order denying the petition for rehearing. If a timely notice of appeal is filed by a party, any other party may file a notice of appeal within ten days after the first notice of appeal was filed. A petition prepared in accordance with Rule 15(c) for discretionary review in the event the appeal is determined not to be of right or for issues in addition to those set out as the basis for a dissenting opinion may be filed with or contained in the notice of appeal.

(b) Content of Notice of Appeal.

(1) Appeal Based Upon Dissent in Court of Appeals. In an appeal which is based upon the existence of a dissenting opinion in the Court of Appeals, the notice of appeal shall specify the party or parties taking the appeal; shall designate the judgment of the Court of Appeals from which the appeal is taken; shall state the basis upon which it is asserted that appeal lies of right under N.C.G.S. § 7A-30; and shall state the issue or issues which are the basis of the dissenting opinion and which are to be presented to the Supreme Court for review.

(2) Appeal Presenting Constitutional Question. In an appeal which is asserted by the appellant to involve a substantial constitutional question, the notice

---

43   See Appendix D for a Sample Brief

of appeal shall specify the party or parties taking the appeal; shall designate the judgment of the Court of Appeals from which the appeal is taken; shall state the issue or issues which are the basis of the constitutional claim and which are to be presented to the Supreme Court for review; shall specify the articles and sections of the Constitution asserted to be involved; shall state with particularity how appellant's rights thereunder have been violated; and shall affirmatively state that the constitutional issue was timely raised (in the trial tribunal if it could have been, in the Court of Appeals if not) and either not determined or determined erroneously.

(c) Record on Appeal.

(1) Composition. The record on appeal filed in the Court of Appeals constitutes the record on appeal for review by the Supreme Court. However, the Supreme Court may note de novo any deficiencies in the record on appeal and may take such action in respect thereto as it deems appropriate, including dismissal of the appeal.

(2) Transmission; Docketing; Copies. Upon the filing of a notice of appeal, the clerk of the Court of Appeals will forthwith transmit the original record on appeal to the clerk of the Supreme Court, who shall thereupon file the record and docket the appeal. The clerk of the Supreme Court will procure or reproduce copies of the record on appeal for distribution as directed by the Court, and may require a deposit from appellant to cover the cost of reproduction.

(d) Briefs.

(1) Filing and Service; Copies. Within thirty days after filing notice of appeal in the Supreme Court, the appellant shall file with the clerk of the Supreme Court and serve upon all other parties copies of a new brief prepared in conformity with Rule 28, presenting only those issues upon which review by the Supreme Court is sought; provided, however, that when the appeal is based upon the existence of a substantial constitutional question or when the appellant has filed a petition for discretionary review for issues in addition to those set out as the basis of a dissent in the Court of Appeals, the appellant shall file and serve a new brief within thirty days after entry of the order of the Supreme Court which determines for the purpose of retaining the appeal on the docket that a substantial constitutional question does exist or allows or denies the petition for discretionary review in an appeal based upon a dissent. Within thirty days

after service of the appellant's brief upon appellee, the appellee shall similarly file and serve copies of a new brief. If permitted by Rule 28(h), the appellant may serve and file a reply brief as provided in that rule.

The parties need file but single copies of their respective briefs. The clerk will reproduce and distribute copies as directed by the Court, billing the parties pursuant to these rules.

(2) Failure to File or Serve. If an appellant fails to file and serve its brief within the time allowed, the appeal may be dismissed on motion of an appellee or on the Court's own initiative. If an appellee fails to file and serve its brief within the time allowed, it may not be heard in oral argument except by permission of the Court.

CHAPTER NINE: SCOPE OF APPELLATE REVIEW

RULE 15: Discretionary Review on Certification By Supreme Court Under G.S. § 7A-31.

Rule 15 addresses discretionary appeals to the N.C. Supreme Court pursuant to N.C.G.S. § 7A-31. Under Rule 15(a), any party to an appeal may file a petition for discretionary review with the Supreme Court either before or after the Court of Appeals dockets an appeal or makes a determination in a case.

Rule 15(b) establishes the time in which the appellant may file a petition for discretionary review. If the appeal is taken before the Court of Appeals issues its decision, the petition must be filed and served within 15 days after the Court of Appeals has docketed the case. If, on the other hand, the appeal is filed after the Court of Appeals issues its decision, the petition must be filed within 15 days after the Court of Appeals has issued its mandate to the trial court. Rule 31, below, addresses when a mandate is issued.

In either case, the petition for discretionary review may be filed with a notice of appeal of right so as to address those issues that are not appealable of right. Appellants often file both a petition for discretionary review and notice of appeal on issues that are, debatably, not proper for automatic appeal. As with appeals of right, a petition for rehearing in the Court of Appeals tolls the running of the 15 days to file the petition. The time starts to run again when the Court of Appeals enters an order on the petition to rehear. See Rule 31 for rehearing petitions

Rule 15(c) states the following required contents for a petition for discretionary review: (1) Plain and concise statement of the factual and legal bases for review under N.C.G.S. § 7A-31 for each issue upon which the appellant seeks review and (2) "each question for which review is sought." The petitioner must also attach a copy of the Court of Appeals' opinion if the petition is filed after that opinion is issued. The petitioner is not required to file a supporting brief but can cite authorities in support of the petition "briefly" in the petition.

Rule 15(d) covers the response to a petition for discretionary review. As the appellee, counsel must respond within 10 days from the date that a timely petition for discretionary review has been filed. Rule 15 does not permit an appellee to raise its own issues for review after the 10 days has elapsed for a response to the petition. And, keep in mind, no extensions of time are provided for the response.

(a) Petition of Party. Either prior to or following determination by the Court of Appeals of an appeal docketed in that court, any party to the appeal may in writing petition the Supreme Court upon any grounds specified in N.C.G.S. § 7A-31 to certify the cause for discretionary review by the Supreme Court; except that a petition for discretionary review of an appeal from the Industrial Commission, the North Carolina State Bar, the Property Tax Commission, the Board of State Contract Appeals, or the Commissioner of Insurance may only be made following determination by the Court of Appeals; and except that no petition for discretionary review may be filed in any postconviction proceeding under N.C.G.S. Ch. 15A, Art. 89, or in valuation of exempt property under N.C.G.S. Ch. 1C.

(b) Same; Filing and Service. A petition for review prior to determination by the Court of Appeals shall be filed with the clerk of the Supreme Court and served on all other parties within fifteen days after the appeal is docketed in the Court of Appeals. For cases that arise from the Industrial Commission, a copy of the petition shall be served on the Chair of the Industrial Commission. A petition for review following determination by the Court of Appeals shall be similarly filed and served within fifteen days after the mandate of the Court of Appeals has been issued to the trial tribunal. Such a petition may be contained in or filed with a notice of appeal of right, to be considered by the Supreme Court in the event the appeal is determined not to be of right, as provided in Rule 14(a). The running of the time for filing and serving a petition for review following determination by the Court of Appeals is terminated as to all parties by the filing by any party within such time of a petition for rehearing under Rule 31 of these rules, and the full time for filing and serving such a petition for review thereafter commences to run and is computed as to all parties from the date of entry by the Court of Appeals of an order denying the petition for rehearing. If a timely petition for review is filed by a party, any other party may file a petition for review within ten days after the first petition for review was filed.

(c) Same; Content. The petition shall designate the petitioner or petitioners and shall set forth plainly and concisely the factual and legal basis upon which it is asserted that grounds exist under N.C.G.S. § 7A-31 for discretionary review. The petition shall state each issue for which review is sought and shall be accompanied by a copy of the opinion of the Court of Appeals when filed after determination by that court. No supporting brief is required, but supporting authorities may be set forth briefly in the petition.

(d) Response. A response to the petition may be filed by any other party within ten days after service of the petition upon that party. No supporting brief is required, but supporting authorities may be set forth briefly in the response. If, in the event that the Supreme Court certifies the case for review, the respondent would seek to present issues in addition to those presented by the petitioner, those additional issues shall be stated in the response. A motion for extension of time is not permitted.

(e) Certification by Supreme Court; How Determined and Ordered.

(1) On Petition of a Party. The determination by the Supreme Court whether to certify for review upon petition of a party is made solely upon the petition and any response thereto and without oral argument.

(2) On Initiative of the Court. The determination by the Supreme Court whether to certify for review upon its own initiative pursuant to N.C.G.S. § 7A-31 is made without prior notice to the parties and without oral argument.

(3) Orders; Filing and Service. Any determination to certify for review and any determination not to certify made in response to a petition will be recorded by the Supreme Court in a written order. The clerk of the Supreme Court will forthwith enter such order, deliver a copy thereof to the clerk of the Court of Appeals, and mail copies to all parties. The cause is docketed in the Supreme Court upon entry of an order of certification by the clerk of the Supreme Court.

(f) Record on Appeal.

(1) Composition. The record on appeal filed in the Court of Appeals constitutes the record on appeal for review by the Supreme Court. However, the Supreme Court may note de novo any deficiencies in the record on appeal and may take

such action in respect thereto as it deems appropriate, including dismissal of the appeal.

(2) Filing; Copies. When an order of certification is filed with the clerk of the Court of Appeals, he or she will forthwith transmit the original record on appeal to the clerk of the Supreme Court. The clerk of the Supreme Court will procure or reproduce copies thereof for distribution as directed by the Court. If it is necessary to reproduce copies, the clerk may require a deposit by the petitioner to cover the costs thereof.

(g) Filing and Service of Briefs.

(1) Cases Certified Before Determination by Court of Appeals. When a case is certified for review by the Supreme Court before being determined by the Court of Appeals, the times allowed the parties by Rule 13 to file their respective briefs are not thereby extended. If a party has filed its brief in the Court of Appeals and served copies before the case is certified, the clerk of the Court of Appeals shall forthwith transmit to the clerk of the Supreme Court the original brief and any copies already reproduced for distribution, and if filing was timely in the Court of Appeals this constitutes timely filing in the Supreme Court. If a party has not filed its brief in the Court of Appeals and served copies before the case is certified, the party shall file its brief in the Supreme Court and serve copies within the time allowed and in the manner provided by Rule 13 for filing and serving in the Court of Appeals.

(2) Cases Certified for Review of Court of Appeals Determinations. When a case is certified for review by the Supreme Court of a determination made by the Court of Appeals, the appellant shall file a new brief prepared in conformity with Rule 28 in the Supreme Court and serve copies upon all other parties within thirty days after the case is docketed in the Supreme Court by entry of its order of certification. The appellee shall file a new brief in the Supreme Court and serve copies upon all other parties within thirty days after a copy of appellant's brief is served upon the appellee. If permitted by Rule 28(h), the appellant may serve and file a reply brief as provided in that rule.

(3) Copies. A party need file, or the clerk of the Court of Appeals transmit, but a single copy of any brief required by this Rule 15 to be filed in the Supreme Court upon certification for discretionary review. The clerk of the Supreme Court will thereupon procure from the Court of Appeals or will reproduce

copies for distribution as directed by the Supreme Court. The clerk may require a deposit by any party to cover the costs of reproducing copies of its brief.

In civil appeals in forma pauperis a party need not pay the deposit for reproducing copies, but at the time of filing its original new brief shall also deliver to the clerk two legible copies thereof.

(4) Failure to File or Serve. If an appellant fails to file and serve its brief within the time allowed by this Rule 15, the appeal may be dismissed on motion of an appellee or upon the Court's own initiative. If an appellee fails to file and serve its brief within the time allowed by this Rule 15, it may not be heard in oral argument except by permission of the Court.

(h) Discretionary Review of Interlocutory Orders. An interlocutory order by the Court of Appeals, including an order for a new trial or for further proceedings in the trial tribunal, will be certified for review by the Supreme Court only upon a determination by the Court that failure to certify would cause a delay in final adjudication which would probably result in substantial harm to a party.

(i) Appellant, Appellee Defined. As used in this Rule 15, the terms "appellant" and "appellee" have the following meanings:

(1) With respect to Supreme Court review prior to determination by the Court of Appeals, whether on petition of a party or on the Court's own initiative, "appellant" means a party who appealed from the trial tribunal; "appellee" means a party who did not appeal from the trial tribunal.

(2) With respect to Supreme Court review of a determination of the Court of Appeals, whether on petition of a party or on the Court's own initiative, "appellant" means the party aggrieved by the determination of the Court of Appeals; "appellee" means the opposing party; provided that, in its order of certification, the Supreme Court may designate either party an appellant or appellee for purposes of proceeding under this Rule 15.

RULE 16: Scope of Review of Decisions of Court of Appeals

Rule 16 describes the function of the Supreme Court on appeal. Whether the appeal is granted as "of right" or under discretionary review, the Court's role, as defined in Rule 16(a), will be to determine "whether there is error of law in the decision of the Court of Appeals." The Court reviews only that decision. *See Falls Sales Co. v. Board of Transp.*, 292 N.C. 437, 443, 233 S.E.2d 569, 573 (1977) (appellant did not assign error to directed verdict in its brief to the Court of Appeals, and therefore, it could not be raised on appeal to Supreme Court). Generally, review is limited to the questions raised in the petition and in the response to the petition, although the Court may, on its own accord, further limit review.

If the appeal is based solely on dissent in the Court of Appeals, then under Rule 16(b), the Supreme Court's review will be limited to questions that are (1) specifically set out in the dissenting opinion, (2) which are stated in the notice of appeal and (3) which are properly presented in the new briefs filed in the Supreme Court. Rule 16(c) explains how parties are designated as "appellant" and "appellee" in the Supreme Court, which is self-explanatory.

(a) How Determined. Review by the Supreme Court after a determination by the Court of Appeals, whether by appeal of right or by discretionary review, is to determine whether there is error of law in the decision of the Court of Appeals. Except when the appeal is based solely upon the existence of a dissent in the Court of Appeals, review in the Supreme Court is limited to consideration of the issues stated in the notice of appeal filed pursuant to Rule 14(b)(2) or the petition for discretionary review and the response thereto filed pursuant to Rule 15(c) and (d), unless further limited by the Supreme Court, and properly presented in the new briefs required by Rules 14(d)(1) and 15(g)(2) to be filed in the Supreme Court.

(b) Scope of Review in Appeal Based Solely Upon Dissent. When the sole ground of the appeal of right is the existence of a dissent in the Court of Appeals, review by the Supreme Court is limited to a consideration of those issues that are (1) specifically set out in the dissenting opinion as the basis for that dissent, (2) stated in the notice of appeal, and (3) properly presented in the new briefs required by Rule 14(d)(1) to be filed in the Supreme Court. Other issues in the case may properly be presented to the Supreme Court through a petition for discretionary review pursuant to Rule 15, or by petition for writ of certiorari pursuant to Rule 21.

(c) Appellant, Appellee Defined. As used in this Rule 16, the terms "appellant" and "appellee" have the following meanings when applied to discretionary review:

(1) With respect to Supreme Court review of a determination of the Court of Appeals upon petition of a party, "appellant" means the petitioner and "appellee" means the respondent.

(2) With respect to Supreme Court review upon the Court's own initiative, "appellant" means the party aggrieved by the decision of the Court of Appeals and "appellee" means the opposing party; provided that, in its order of certification, the Supreme Court may designate either party an "appellant" or "appellee" for purposes of proceeding under this Rule 16.

RULE 17: Appeal Bond in Appeals Under G.S. § 7A-30, 7A-31.

Rule 17 addresses bond in appeals from the Court of Appeals to the Supreme Court. For GAL purposes, this rule is relevant because it exempts from the bond requirement all appeals that are in forma pauperis.

(a) Appeal of Right. In all appeals of right from the Court of Appeals to the Supreme Court in civil cases, the party who takes appeal shall, upon filing the notice of appeal in the Supreme Court, file with the clerk of that Court a written undertaking, with good and sufficient surety in the sum of $250, or deposit cash in lieu thereof, to the effect that all costs awarded against the appealing party on the appeal will be paid.

(b) Discretionary Review of Court of Appeals Determination. When the Supreme Court on petition of a party certifies a civil case for review of a determination of the Court of Appeals, the petitioner shall file an undertaking for costs in the form provided in subsection (a). When the Supreme Court on its own initiative certifies a case for review of a determination of the Court of Appeals, no undertaking for costs shall be required of any party.

(c) Discretionary Review by Supreme Court Before Court of Appeals Determination. When a civil case is certified for review by the Supreme Court before being determined by the Court of Appeals, the undertaking on appeal initially filed in the Court of Appeals shall stand for the payment of all costs incurred in either the Court of Appeals or the Supreme Court and awarded against the party appealing.

(d) Appeals in Forma Pauperis. No undertakings for costs are required of a party appealing in forma pauperis

RULE 18: Taking Appeal; Record on Appeal – Composition and Settlement.

Rule 18 discusses the special procedures when an appellant is appealing an order directly from an administrative agency to the Court of Appeals. For example, all Industrial Commission opinions appeal directly to the Court of Appeals after all administrative remedies are exhausted. In general, the appellate steps are the same as those taken when appealing from the superior court. Nonetheless, once the appeal goes to the Court of Appeals, administrative appellate parties must take the following steps:

(a) General. Appeals of right from administrative agencies, boards, or commissions (hereinafter "agency") directly to the appellate division under N.C.G.S. § 7A-29 shall be in accordance with the procedures provided in these rules for appeals of right from the courts of the trial divisions, except as provided in this Article.

(b) Time and Method for Taking Appeals.

(1) The times and methods for taking appeals from an agency shall be as provided in this Rule 18 unless the statutes governing the agency provide otherwise, in which case those statutes shall control.

(2) Any party to the proceeding may appeal from a final agency determination to the appropriate court of the appellate division for alleged errors of law by filing and serving a notice of appeal within thirty days after receipt of a copy of the final order of the agency. The final order of the agency is to be sent to the parties by Registered or Certified Mail. The notice of appeal shall specify the party or parties taking the appeal; shall designate the final agency determination from which appeal is taken and the court to which appeal is taken; and shall be signed by counsel of record for the party or parties taking the appeal, or by any such party not represented by counsel of record.

(3) If a transcript of fact-finding proceedings is not made by the agency as part of the process leading up to the final agency determination, the appealing party may contract with the reporter for production of such parts of the proceedings not already on file as it deems necessary, pursuant to the procedures prescribed in Rule 7.

(c) Composition of Record on Appeal. The record on appeal in appeals from any agency shall contain:

(1) an index of the contents of the record on appeal, which shall appear as the first page thereof;

(2) a statement identifying the commission or agency from whose judgment, order, or opinion appeal is taken; the session at which the judgment, order, or opinion was rendered, or if rendered out of session, the time and place of rendition; and the party appealing;

(3) a copy of the summons with return, notice of hearing, or other papers showing jurisdiction of the agency over persons or property sought to be bound in the proceeding, or a statement showing same;

(4) copies of all other notices, pleadings, petitions, or other papers required by law or rule of the agency to be filed with the agency to present and define the matter for determination, including a Form 44 for all workers' compensation cases which originate from the Industrial Commission;

(5) a copy of any findings of fact and conclusions of law and a copy of the order, award, decision, or other determination of the agency from which appeal was taken;

(6) so much of the litigation before the agency or before any division, commissioner, deputy commissioner, or hearing officer of the agency, set out in the form provided in Rule 9(c)(1), as is necessary for an understanding of all issues presented on appeal, or a statement specifying that the verbatim transcript of proceedings is being filed with the record pursuant to Rule 9(c)(2) and (c)(3);

(7) when the agency has reviewed a record of proceedings before a division or an individual commissioner, deputy commissioner, or hearing officer of the

agency, copies of all items included in the record filed with the agency which are necessary for an understanding of all issues presented on appeal;

(8) copies of all other papers filed and statements of all other proceedings had before the agency or any of its individual commissioners, deputies, or divisions which are necessary to an understanding of all issues presented on appeal, unless they appear in the verbatim transcript of proceedings being filed pursuant to Rule 9(c)(2) and (c)(3);

(9) a copy of the notice of appeal from the agency, of all orders establishing time limits relative to the perfecting of the appeal, of any order finding a party to the appeal to be a civil pauper, and of any agreement, notice of approval, or order settling the record on appeal and settling the verbatim transcript of proceedings if one is filed pursuant to Rule 9(c)(2) and (c)(3);

(10) proposed issues on appeal relating to the actions of the agency, set out as provided in Rule 10;

(11) a statement, when appropriate, that the record of proceedings was made with an electronic recording device;

(12) a statement, when appropriate, that a supplement compiled pursuant to Rule 18(d)(3) is filed with the record on appeal; and

(13) any order (issued prior to the filing of the record on appeal) ruling upon any motion by an attorney who is not licensed to practice law in North Carolina to be admitted pursuant to N.C.G.S. § 84-4.1 to appear in the appeal. In the event such a motion is filed prior to the filing of the record but has not yet been ruled upon when the record is filed, the record shall include a statement that such a motion is pending and the date that motion was filed.

(d) Settling the Record on Appeal. The record on appeal may be settled by any of the following methods:

(1) By Agreement. Within thirty-five days after filing of the notice of appeal, or after production of the transcript if one is ordered pursuant to Rule 18(b)(3), the parties may by agreement entered in the record on appeal settle a proposed record on appeal prepared by any party in accordance with this Rule 18 as the record on appeal.

(2) By Appellee's Approval of Appellant's Proposed Record on Appeal. If the record on appeal is not settled by agreement under Rule 18(d)(1), the appellant shall, within thirty-five days after filing of the notice of appeal, or after production of the transcript if one is ordered pursuant to Rule 18(b)(3), serve upon all other parties a proposed record on appeal constituted in accordance with the provisions of Rule 18(c). Within thirty days after service of the proposed record on appeal upon an appellee, that appellee may serve upon all other parties a notice of approval of the proposed record on appeal or objections, amendments, or a proposed alternative record on appeal. Amendments or objections to the proposed record on appeal shall be set out in a separate paper and shall specify any item(s) for which an objection is based on the contention that the item was not filed, served, submitted for consideration, admitted, or made the subject of an offer of proof, or that the content of a statement or narration is factually inaccurate. An appellant who objects to an appellee's response to the proposed record on appeal shall make the same specification in its request for judicial settlement. The formatting of the proposed record on appeal and the order in which items appear in it is the responsibility of the appellant. Judicial settlement is not appropriate for disputes concerning only the formatting or the order in which items appear in the settled record on appeal. If all appellees within the times allowed them either file notices of approval or fail to file either notices of approval or objections, amendments, or proposed alternative records on appeal, appellant's proposed record on appeal thereupon constitutes the record on appeal.

(3) By Agreement, by Operation of Rule, or by Court Order After Appellee's Objection or Amendment. If any appellee timely files amendments, objections, or a proposed alternative record on appeal, the record on appeal shall consist of each item that is either among those items required by Rule 9(a) to be in the record on appeal or that is requested by any party to the appeal and agreed upon for inclusion by all other parties to the appeal, in the absence of contentions that the item was not filed, served, or offered into evidence. If a party requests that an item be included in the record on appeal but not all parties to the appeal agree to its inclusion, then that item shall not be included in the printed record on appeal, but shall be filed by the appellant with the record on appeal in a volume captioned "Rule 18(d)(3) Supplement to the Printed Record on Appeal," along with any verbatim transcripts, narrations of proceedings, documentary exhibits, and other items that are filed pursuant to Rule 18(b) or 18(c); provided that any item not filed, served, submitted for

consideration, admitted, or for which no offer of proof was tendered shall not be included. Subject to the additional requirements of Rule 28(d), items in the Rule 18(d)(3) supplement may be cited and used by the parties as would items in the printed record on appeal.

If a party does not agree to the wording of a statement or narration required or permitted by these rules, there shall be no judicial settlement to resolve the dispute unless the objection is based on a contention that the statement or narration concerns an item that was not filed, served, submitted for consideration, admitted, or tendered in an offer of proof, or that a statement or narration is factually inaccurate. Instead, the objecting party is permitted to have inserted in the settled record on appeal a concise counter-statement. Parties are strongly encouraged to reach agreement on the wording of statements in records on appeal.

The Rule 18(d)(3) supplement to the printed record on appeal shall contain an index of the contents of the supplement, which shall appear as the first page thereof. The Rule 18(d)(3) supplement shall be paginated consecutively with the pages of the record on appeal, the first page of the supplement to bear the next consecutive number following the number of the last page of the record on appeal. These pages shall be referred to as "record supplement pages," and shall be cited as "(R. S. p. ___)." The contents of the supplement should be arranged, so far as practicable, in the order in which they occurred or were filed in the trial tribunal. If a party does not agree to the inclusion or specification of an exhibit or transcript in the printed record, the printed record shall include a statement that such items are separately filed along with the supplement.

If any party to the appeal contends that materials proposed for inclusion in the record or for filing therewith pursuant to Rule 18(b) or 18(c) were not filed, served, submitted for consideration, admitted, or offered into evidence, or that a statement or narration permitted by these rules is not factually accurate, then that party, within ten days after expiration of the time within which the appellee last served with the appellant's proposed record on appeal might have filed amendments, objections, or a proposed alternative record on appeal, may in writing request that the agency head convene a conference to settle the record on appeal. A copy of that request, endorsed with a certificate showing service on the agency head, shall be served upon all other parties. Each party shall promptly provide to the agency head a reference copy of the record items, amendments, or objections served by that party in the case.

The functions of the agency head in the settlement of the record on appeal are to determine whether a statement permitted by these rules is not factually accurate, to settle narrations of proceedings under Rule 18(c)(6), and to determine whether the record accurately reflects material filed, served, submitted for consideration, admitted, or made the subject of an offer of proof, but not to decide whether material desired in the record by either party is relevant to the issues on appeal, non-duplicative, or otherwise suited for inclusion in the record on appeal.

Upon receipt of a request for settlement of the record on appeal, the agency head shall send written notice to counsel for all parties setting a place and time for a conference to settle the record on appeal. The conference shall be held not later than fifteen days after service of the request upon the agency head. The agency head or a delegate appointed in writing by the agency head shall settle the record on appeal by order entered not more than twenty days after service of the request for settlement upon the agency. If requested, the settling official shall return the record items submitted for reference during the settlement process with the order settling the record on appeal.

When the agency head is a party to the appeal, the agency head shall forthwith request the Chief Judge of the Court of Appeals or the Chief Justice of the Supreme Court, as appropriate, to appoint a referee to settle the record on appeal. The referee so appointed shall proceed after conference with all parties to settle the record on appeal in accordance with the terms of these rules and the appointing order.

If any appellee timely serves amendments, objections, or a proposed alternative record on appeal, and no judicial settlement of the record is sought, the record is deemed settled as of the expiration of the ten day period within which any party could have requested judicial settlement of the record on appeal under this Rule 18(d)(3).

Nothing herein shall prevent settlement of the record on appeal by agreement of the parties at any time within the times herein limited for settling the record by agency order.

(e) Further Procedures and Additional Materials in the Record on Appeal. Further procedures for perfecting and prosecuting the appeal shall be as provided by these rules for appeals from the courts of the trial divisions.

(f) Extensions of Time. The times provided in this rule for taking any action may be extended in accordance with the provisions of Rule 27(c).

RULE 19: [RESERVED FOR FUTURE USE]

RULE 20: Miscellaneous Provisions of Law Governing in Agency Appeals.

"Specific provisions of law pertaining to stays pending appeals from any agency to the appellate division, to pauper appeals therein, and to the scope of review and permissible mandates of the Court of Appeals therein shall govern the procedure in such appeals notwithstanding any provisions of these rules which may prescribe a different procedure."

CHAPTER TEN: EXTRAORDINARY WRITS

RULE 21: Certiorari

Rules 21(a)(1) and (2) discuss when the Court of Appeals and Supreme Court may issue a writ of *certiorari*, which is an order to the lower court to deliver the record in the case for review. Either court may issue a writ of *certiorari* in three situations: (1) Where a party's right to an appeal "has been lost by failure to take timely action" (*i.e.* where the appellant missed the deadline to file notice of appeal); (2) Where there is no right to appeal from a particular interlocutory order; or (3) Pursuant to N.C.G.S. 15A-1422(c)(3), where the trial court has denied an order for appropriate relief.

Rules 21(b) and (c) address the filing and content requirements of a petition for a writ of *certiorari* as well as which court should receive the petition. Under Rule 21(b), the petition should be filed in the appellate court to which an appeal "might lie from final judgment." While Rule 21(c) does not impose a time limitation for filing the petition, it does state that it "shall be filed without unreasonable delay." The petition must also be accompanied by proof of service upon all parties. The petition for writ of certiorari must contain the following: (1) statement of facts, (2) statement of reasons why the writ should be issued and (3) certified copies of the judgment, order or portions of the record which are necessary to an understanding of the matters presented in the petition. Counsel or petitioner must verify the petition.

Rule 21(d) allows other parties to respond to the petition within ten days of service. If needed, these responses must be accompanied by affidavits or certified copies of documents not filed with the original petition. The response must also include proof of service of the response on all parties. No brief or oral argument is allowed in response to a petition for writ of *certiorari* unless the appellate court so orders.

Appellants who miss the deadline to file notice of appeal often file a petition for discretionary review that asks the appellate court, alternatively, to consider the petition as a petition for a writ of *certiorari*. *See In re I.S.*, 170 N.C. App. 78, 611 S.E.2d 467 (2005) (in termination of parental rights case, even though notice of appeal did not comply with N.C.G.S. § 7B-1113 and N.C. R. App. P. 3, the court treated the petition as a request for a writ of certiorari because a mistake regarding the order appealed from was merely a scrivener's error). When responding to such a petition, counsel should confirm that the petitioner has met all the Rule 21 requirements. If the petitioner has not, then counsel should move to dismiss the appeal for (1) failure to file timely notice of appeal and/or (2) failure to follow the rule's requirements. *See State v. McCoy*, 171 N.C. App. 636, 637, 615 S.E.2d 319, 321 (2005) (where petitioner failed to file timely notice of appeal, the appellate court had discretion to hear issues on their merits by granting writ of *certiorari*; however, a mere footnote in the petitioner's brief did not satisfy the statement of facts requirement of Rule 21(c)). Although no time limitation is imposed, counsel opposing the writ of *certiorari* can also raise the doctrine of laches or a similar argument. *See Stone v. Ledbetter*, 191 N.C. 777, 779, 133 S.E. 162, 163 (1926)(holding that petitioner must show itself free from laches by doing all in its power towards having the appeal perfected and docketed in time).

All counsel should seriously consider responding to a petition for writ of *certiorari*. The response should be brief but include enough information for the appellate court to make a determination. Even if the appellate court grants the writ and requests oral argument, the court may later dismiss the writ as "improvidently granted."

(a) Scope of the Writ.

(1) Review of the Judgments and Orders of Trial Tribunals. The writ of certiorari may be issued in appropriate circumstances by either appellate court to permit review of the judgments and orders of trial tribunals when the right to prosecute an appeal has been lost by failure to take timely action, or when no right of appeal from an interlocutory order exists, or for review pursuant to N.C.G.S. § 15A-1422(c)(3) of an order of the trial court denying a motion for appropriate relief.

(2) Review of the Judgments and Orders of the Court of Appeals. The writ of certiorari may be issued by the Supreme Court in appropriate circumstances to permit review of the decisions and orders of the Court of Appeals when the right to prosecute an appeal of right or to petition for discretionary review has been lost by failure to take timely action, or for review of orders of the Court of Appeals when no right of appeal exists.

(b) Petition for Writ; to Which Appellate Court Addressed. Application for the writ of certiorari shall be made by filing a petition therefor with the clerk of the court of the appellate division to which appeal of right might lie from a final judgment in the cause by the tribunal to which issuance of the writ is sought.

(c) Same; Filing and Service; Content. The petition shall be filed without unreasonable delay and shall be accompanied by proof of service upon all other parties. For cases which arise from the Industrial Commission, a copy of the petition shall be served on the Chair of the Industrial Commission. The petition shall contain a statement of the facts necessary to an understanding of the issues presented by the application; a statement of the reasons why the writ should issue; and certified copies of the judgment, order, or opinion or parts of the record which may be essential to an understanding of the matters set forth in the petition. The petition shall be verified by counsel or the petitioner. Upon receipt of the prescribed docket fee, the clerk will docket the petition.

(d) Response; Determination by Court. Within ten days after service of the petition any party may file a response thereto with supporting affidavits or certified portions of the record not filed with the petition. Filing shall be accompanied by proof of service upon all other parties. The court for good cause shown may shorten the time for filing a response. Determination will be made on the basis of the petition, the response, and any supporting papers. No briefs or oral argument will be received or allowed unless ordered by the court upon its own initiative.

(e) Petition for Writ in Postconviction Matters; to Which Appellate Court Addressed. Petitions for writ of certiorari to review orders of the trial court denying motions for appropriate relief upon grounds listed in N.C.G.S. § 15A-1415(b) by persons who have been convicted of murder in the first degree and sentenced to death shall be filed in the Supreme Court. In all other cases such petitions shall be filed in and determined by the Court of Appeals, and the Supreme Court will not entertain petitions for certiorari or petitions for further discretionary review in these cases. In the event the petitioner unreasonably delays in filing the petition or otherwise fails to comply with a rule of procedure, the petition shall be dismissed by the court. If the petition is without merit, it shall be denied by the court.

(f) Petition for Writ in Postconviction Matters--Death Penalty Cases. A petition for writ of certiorari to review orders of the trial court on motions for appropriate relief in death penalty cases shall be filed in the Supreme Court within sixty days after delivery of the transcript of the hearing on the motion for appropriate relief to the petitioning party. The responding party shall file its response within thirty days of service of the petition.

RULE 22: Mandamus and Prohibition.

Rules 22(a) and (b) address the filing and content requirements of a petition for mandamus or prohibition as well as which court should receive the petition. Under Rule 22(a), the petition should be addressed to the appellate court to which an appeal "might lie from final judgment," which means a final judgment on the merits of the case that are not open for future adjudication. *See In re C.E.L.*, 171 N.C. App. 468, 478, 615 S.E.2d 427, 432 (2005) (permanency planning order giving temporary, nonprejudicial custody of child to aunt was not a final judgment and did not prevent court from ordering the termination of parental rights).

Rule 22(b), like its Rule 21 counterpart, does not impose a time limit for filing the petition but instead states that the petition for a writ of mandamus or prohibition must be filed "without unreasonable delay" after the judicial action at issue has occurred. Because these writs affect the trial court's actions, the petition must be accompanied by proof of service of the petition upon the respondent judge (or judges) as well as all parties to the action.

Petitions for writs of mandamus and prohibition must contain: (1) statement of the facts, (2) statement of the issues and relief sought, (3) statement of the reasons why the writ should be issued and (4) certified copies of the opinion, order or portions of the record that are necessary to an understanding of the matters presented in the petition. Counsel or petitioner must verify the petition.

Rule 22(c) allows other parties to respond to the petition within 10 days of service. If needed, these responses must be accompanied by affidavits or certified copies of documents not filed with the original petition. The response must also include proof of service of the response on all parties. The rule does not allow a brief or oral argument in response to a petition for writ of mandamus or prohibition unless the appellate court so orders.

(a) Petition for writ; To which appellate court addressed.
Applications for the writs of mandamus or prohibition directed to a judge, judges, commissioner, or commissioners shall be made by filing a petition therefor with the clerk of the court to which appeal of right might lie from a final judgment entered in the cause by the judge, judges, commissioner, or commissioners to whom issuance of the writ is sought.

(b) Same; Filing and service; Content.

The petition shall be filed without unreasonable delay after the judicial action sought to be prohibited or compelled has been undertaken, or has occurred, or has been refused, and shall be accompanied by proof of service on the respondent judge, judges, commissioner, or commissioners and on all other parties to the action. The petition shall contain a statement of the facts necessary to an understanding of the issues presented by the application; a statement of the issues presented and of the relief sought; a statement of the reasons why the writ should issue; and certified copies of any order or opinion or parts of the record which may be essential to an understanding of the matters set forth in the petition. The petition shall be verified by counsel or the petitioner. Upon receipt of the prescribed docket fee, the clerk shall docket the petition.

(c) Response; Determination by court.

Within 10 days after service upon him of the petition the respondent or any party may file a response thereto with supporting affidavits or certified portions of the record not filed with the petition. Filing shall be accompanied by proof of service upon all other parties. The Court for good cause shown may shorten the time for filing a response. Determination will be made on the basis of the petition, the response and any supporting papers. No briefs or oral argument will be received or allowed unless ordered by the court upon its own initiative.

RULE 23: Supersedeas.

A writ of supersedeas stays the execution of judgments, orders or other trial court determinations where an action is not automatically stayed by filing an appeal or a petition for writ of certiorari, mandamus or prohibition. Rule 23 covers the writ of supersedeas, which has requirements similar to those of the other extraordinary writs. Writs of supersedeas essentially fall into two categories: (1) those based on trial court proceedings; and (2) those based on appeals in the Court of Appeals.

Rule 23(a) addresses the petition for writ of supersedeas that arises from the trial court proceedings. The party seeking the writ must have either (1) motioned the trial court for a stay or (2) demonstrated "extraordinary circumstances" which render a motion for a stay to the trial court "impracticable." Unless the Supreme Court initially dockets the case, the writ of supersedeas must be made to the Court of Appeals.

Rule 23(b) addresses the writ of supersedeas that arises from a decision of the Court of Appeals. In this case, no motion for a stay in the Court of Appeals is necessary before petitioning the Supreme Court. Rule 23(c) describes the requirements for the petition. Similar to the other extraordinary writs, the petition must be verified and accompanied by proof of service on all parties to the action. If the petition is filed in the Court of Appeals, it must include a statement showing either: (1) the impracticability of a motion for a stay in the trial court; or (2) the order granting or denying the stay. Rule 23(c) also requires the following contents: (1) statement of facts needed to understand the basis upon which the writ is sought; (2) statement of the reasons why the court should issue the writ "in justice to the applicant;" and (3) supporting affidavits and certified portions of the record that support issuance of the writ.

Rule 23(d) permits other parties to respond to the petition within 10 days of service. Responses must be accompanied by affidavits or certified copies of documents not filed with the original petition as needed. The response must include proof of service of the response on all parties. The rule does not allow a brief or oral argument in response to a petition for writ of supersedeas unless the appellate court so orders.

Under Rule 23(e), applicants for a writ of supersedeas may also apply for a temporary stay of enforcement of the underlying order. This application can be made separately or in the petition for writ of mandamus. If the application for temporary stay is made separately from the petition for writ of mandamus, the application must comport with the filing and service requirements of Rule 23. This order may be issued ex parte. Counsel may include a petition for writ of supersedeas in a petition for discretionary review to the Supreme Court or in a petition for writ of certiorari, mandamus or prohibition that is made to either the Court of Appeals or Supreme Court.

(a) Pending Review of Trial Tribunal Judgments and Orders.

(1) Application--When Appropriate. Application may be made to the appropriate appellate court for a writ of supersedeas to stay the execution or enforcement of any judgment, order, or other determination of a trial tribunal which is not automatically stayed by the taking of appeal when an appeal has been taken, or a petition for mandamus, prohibition, or certiorari has been filed to obtain review of the judgment, order, or other determination; and (i) a stay order or entry has been sought by the applicant by deposit of security or by motion in the trial tribunal and such order or entry has been denied or vacated by the trial tribunal, or (ii) extraordinary circumstances make it impracticable to obtain a stay by deposit of security or by application to the trial tribunal for a stay order.

(2) Same--How and to Which Appellate Court Made. Application for the writ is by petition which shall in all cases, except those initially docketed in the Supreme Court, be first made to the Court of Appeals. Except when an appeal from a superior court is initially docketed in the Supreme Court, no petition will be entertained by the Supreme Court unless application has been made first to the Court of Appeals and denied by that Court.

(b) Pending Review by Supreme Court of Court of Appeals Decisions. Application may be made in the first instance to the Supreme Court for a writ of supersedeas to stay the execution or enforcement of a judgment, order, or other determination mandated by the Court of Appeals when a notice of appeal of right or a petition for discretionary review has been or will be timely filed, or a petition for review by certiorari, mandamus, or prohibition has been filed to obtain review of the decision of the Court of Appeals. No prior motion for a stay order need be made to the Court of Appeals.

(c) Petition; Filing and Service; Content. The petition shall be filed with the clerk of the court to which application is being made and shall be accompanied by proof of service upon all other parties. The petition shall be verified by counsel or the petitioner. Upon receipt of the required docket fee, the clerk will docket the petition.

For stays of the judgments of trial tribunals, the petition shall contain a statement that stay has been sought in the court to which issuance of the writ is sought and denied or vacated by that court, or shall contain facts showing that it was impracticable there to seek a stay. For stays of any judgment, the petition shall contain: (1) a statement of any facts necessary to an understanding of the basis upon which the writ is sought; and (2) a statement of reasons why the writ should issue in justice to the applicant. The petition may be accompanied by affidavits and by any certified portions of the record pertinent to its consideration. It may be included in a petition for discretionary review by the Supreme Court under N.C.G.S. § 7A-31, or in a petition to either appellate court for certiorari, mandamus, or prohibition.

(d) Response; Determination by Court. Within ten days after service of the petition any party may file a response thereto with supporting affidavits or certified portions of the record not filed with the petition. Filing shall be accompanied by proof of service upon all other parties. The court for good cause shown may shorten the time for filing a response. Determination will be made on the basis of the petition, the response, and any supporting papers. No briefs or oral argument will be received or allowed unless ordered by the court upon its own initiative.

(e) Temporary Stay. Upon the filing of a petition for supersedeas, the applicant may apply, either within the petition or by separate paper, for an order temporarily staying enforcement or execution of the judgment, order, or other determination pending decision by the court upon the petition for supersedeas. If application is made by separate paper, it shall be filed and served in the manner provided for the petition for supersedeas in Rule 23(c). The court for good cause shown in such a petition for temporary stay may issue such an order ex parte. In capital cases, such stay, if granted, shall remain in effect until the period for filing a petition for certiorari in the United States Supreme Court has passed without a petition being filed, or until certiorari on a timely filed petition has been denied by that Court. At that time, the stay shall automatically dissolve.

RULE 24: Form of Papers; Copies.

Rule 24 provides that a party need only file one copy with the clerk of court of any paper filed in connection with an extraordinary writ.

A party need file with the appellate court but a single copy of any paper required to be filed in connection with applications for extraordinary writs. The court may direct that additional copies be filed. The clerk will not reproduce copies.

CHAPTER ELEVEN: GENERAL PROVISIONS

RULE 25: Penalties for Failure to Comply With Rules.

If the appellant files a notice of appeal but then fails to perfect the appeal, the appeal may be dismissed by motion of another party. If the appeal has not been docketed at the Court of Appeals, make the motion at the trial court level. Sanctions are available under Rule 25(b).

(a) Failure of Appellant to Take Timely Action. If after giving notice of appeal from any court, commission, or commissioner the appellant shall fail within the times allowed by these rules or by order of court to take any action required to present the appeal for decision, the appeal may on motion of any other party be dismissed. Prior to the filing of an appeal in an appellate court, motions to dismiss are made to the court, commission, or commissioner from which appeal has been taken; after an appeal has been filed in an appellate court, motions to dismiss are made to that court. Motions to dismiss shall be supported by affidavits or certified copies of docket entries which show the failure to take timely action or otherwise perfect the appeal and shall be allowed unless compliance or a waiver thereof is shown on the record, or unless the appellee shall consent to action out of time, or unless the court for good cause shall permit the action to be taken out of time.

Motions heard under this rule to courts of the trial divisions may be heard and determined by any judge of the particular court specified in Rule 36 of these rules; motions made under this rule to a commission may be heard and determined by the chair of the commission; or if to a commissioner, then by that commissioner. The procedure in all motions made under this rule to trial tribunals shall be that provided for motion practice by the N.C. Rules of Civil Procedure; in all motions made under this rule to courts of the appellate division, the procedure shall be that provided by Rule 37 of these rules.

(b) Sanctions for Failure to Comply with Rules. A court of the appellate division may, on its own initiative or motion of a party, impose a sanction against a party or attorney or both when the court determines that such party or attorney or both substantially failed to comply with these appellate rules. The court may impose sanctions of the type and in the manner prescribed by Rule 34 for frivolous appeals.

RULE 26: Filing and Service.

Rule 26(a)(1) allows parties to file all documents by mail. However, for all TPR appeals where the notice of appeal was filed after 1 May 2006, no electronic filing is available. Instead, the appellate attorney must send one original brief and two copies to the Court of Appeals. The documents should be addressed to the clerk and should be received by the clerk within the applicable time frame. Motions and briefs are deemed filed as of the mailing date.

Rule 26(a)(2) allows for electronic filing. To use this form of filing, go to www.ncappellatecourts.org. The document will be deemed filed as of when it was electronically received. Parties may fax responses and motions only if they have received prior oral approval by the clerk's office and follow up the fax with a mailed copy. No matter what is being filed, a party must serve all documents on the other parties to the action, pursuant to Rule 26(b). In *Hale v. Afro-American Arts Intern., Inc.*, 335 N.C. 231, 231, 436 S.E.2d 588, 588 (1993), the Supreme Court held that failure to serve the notice of appeal is a defect in record analogous to the failure to serve process.

Rule 26(c) states that service can be completed as stated in Rule 4, supra. If a document is electronically filed, the party must still serve the other parties by hand or mail. Rule 26(d) provides that a certificate of service must be attached to every filed document, proving that the document was served on all other parties. Joint parties may be served by serving only one of the joint parties under Rule 26(e). Under Rule 26(f), however, when there are numerous parties, a party can serve only the parties listed in the order appealed from to comply with this rule.

Pursuant to Rule 26(g), documents filed with the appellate courts should be on regular, letter-size 8.5" x 11" paper, except for wills and exhibits. Please note the size of the fonts listed in Rule 28. An index to every document 10 pages or more is required along with a table of authorities. Just after the conclusion, a party must include its name, address and telephone number along with a signature. The signature is not required on electronically filed documents. Juveniles' names and other identifying information must be redacted.

(a) Filing. Papers required or permitted by these rules to be filed in the trial or appellate divisions shall be filed with the clerk of the appropriate court. Filing may be accomplished by mail or by electronic means as set forth in this rule.

(1) Filing by Mail. Filing may be accomplished by mail addressed to the clerk but is not timely unless the papers are received by the clerk within the time fixed for filing, except that motions, responses to petitions, the record on appeal, and briefs shall be deemed filed on the date of mailing, as evidenced by the proof of service.

(2) Filing by Electronic Means. Filing in the appellate courts may be accomplished by electronic means by use of the electronic filing site at www. ncappellatecourts.org. All documents may be filed electronically through the use of this site. A document filed by use of the official electronic web site is deemed filed as of the time that the document is received electronically.

Responses and motions may be filed by facsimile machines, if an oral request for permission to do so has first been tendered to and approved by the clerk of the appropriate appellate court.

In all cases in which a document has been filed by facsimile machine pursuant to this rule, counsel must forward the following items by first class mail, contemporaneously with the transmission: the original signed document, the electronic transmission fee, and the applicable filing fee for the document, if any. The party filing a document by electronic means shall be responsible for all costs of the transmission, and neither they nor the electronic transmission fee may be recovered as costs of the appeal. When a document is filed to the electronic filing site at www.ncappellatecourts.org, counsel may either have his or her account drafted electronically by following the procedures described at the electronic filing site, or counsel must forward the applicable filing fee for the document by first class mail, contemporaneously with the transmission.

(b) Service of All Papers Required. Copies of all papers filed by any party and not required by these rules to be served by the clerk shall, at or before the time of filing, be served on all other parties to the appeal.

(c) Manner of Service. Service may be made in the manner provided for service and return of process in Rule 4 of the N.C. Rules of Civil Procedure and may be so made upon a party or upon its attorney of record. Service may also be made upon a party or its attorney of record by delivering a copy to either or by mailing a copy to the recipient's last known address, or if no address is known, by filing it in the office of the clerk with whom the original paper is filed. Delivery of a copy within this rule means handing it to the attorney or to the party, or leaving it at the attorney's office with a partner or employee. Service by mail is complete upon deposit of the paper enclosed in a postpaid, properly addressed wrapper in a post office or official depository under the exclusive care and custody of the United States Postal Service, or, for those having access to such services, upon deposit with the State Courier Service or Inter-Office Mail. When a document is filed electronically to the official web site, service also may be accomplished electronically by use of the other counsel's correct and current electronic mail address(es), or service may be accomplished in the manner described previously in this subsection.

(d) Proof of Service. Papers presented for filing shall contain an acknowledgment of service by the person served or proof of service in the form of a statement of the date and manner of service and of the names of the persons served, certified by the person who made service. Proof of service shall appear on or be affixed to the papers filed.

(e) Joint Appellants and Appellees. Any paper required by these rules to be served on a party is properly served upon all parties joined in the appeal by service upon any one of them.

(f) Numerous Parties to Appeal Proceeding Separately. When there are unusually large numbers of appellees or appellants proceeding separately, the trial tribunal, upon motion of any party or on its own initiative, may order that any papers required by these rules to be served by a party on all other parties need be served only upon parties designated in the order, and that the filing of such a paper and service thereof upon the parties designated constitutes due notice of it to all other parties. A copy of every such order shall be served upon all parties to the action in such manner and form as the court directs.

(g) Documents Filed with Appellate Courts.

(1) Form of Papers. Papers presented to either appellate court for filing shall be letter size (8 1/2 x 11") with the exception of wills and exhibits. All printed matter must appear in at least 12-point type on unglazed white paper of 16-20 pound substance so as to produce a clear, black image, leaving a margin

of approximately one inch on each side. The body of text shall be presented with double spacing between each line of text. No more than twenty-seven lines of double-spaced text may appear on a page, even if proportional type is used. Lines of text shall be no wider than 6 1/2 inches. The format of all papers presented for filing shall follow the additional instructions found in the appendixes to these rules. The format of briefs shall follow the additional instructions found in Rule 28(j).

(2) Index required. All documents presented to either appellate court other than records on appeal, which in this respect are governed by Rule 9, shall, unless they are less than ten pages in length, be preceded by a subject index of the matter contained therein, with page references, and a table of authorities, i.e., cases (alphabetically arranged), constitutional provisions, statutes, and textbooks cited, with references to the pages where they are cited.

(3) Closing. The body of the document shall at its close bear the printed name, post office address, telephone number, State Bar number and e-mail address of counsel of record, and in addition, at the appropriate place, the manuscript signature of counsel of record. If the document has been filed electronically by use of the official web site at www.ncappellatecourts.org, the manuscript signature of counsel of record is not required.

(4) Protecting the Identity of Certain Juveniles. Parties shall protect the identity of juveniles covered by Rules 3(b)(1), 3.1(b), or 4(e) pursuant to said rules.

RULE 27: Computation and Extension of Time.

Rule 27(a) explains how to compute time as defined in these rules. In computing time, the date of the last act is not included. The last day is counted unless it falls on a weekend or a legal holiday. In that case, use the next business day. When a document is mailed, add three additional days to the prescribed time period, pursuant to Rule 27(b). Under Rule 27(c), a party may move for additional time before the prescribed time period is up. These motions may be made and determined ex parte unless the time period has already passed. Then all parties will have the opportunity to be heard, under Rule 27(d).

Our Supreme Court held that the trial judge could extend, ex parte, the time for the State to serve the record on appeal from a forfeiture judgment, notwithstanding the State's error in calculating initial filing date, since the State had given oral and written notice of a motion to extend time to serve proposed record on appeal and complied with outside time limits in which to file settled record on appeal from the time of oral notice of appeal.[44]

(a) Computation of Time. In computing any period of time prescribed or allowed by these rules, by order of court, or by any applicable statute, the day of the act, event, or default after which the designated period of time begins to run is not included. The last day of the period so computed is to be included, unless it is a Saturday, Sunday, or a legal holiday, in which event the period runs until the end of the next day which is not a Saturday, Sunday, or a legal holiday.

(b) Additional Time After Service by Mail. Except as to filing of notice of appeal pursuant to Rule 3(c), whenever a party has the right to do some act or take some proceedings within a prescribed period after the service of a notice or other paper and the notice or paper is served by mail, three days shall be added to the prescribed period.

(c) Extensions of Time; By Which Court Granted. Except as herein provided, courts for good cause shown may upon motion extend any of the times prescribed by these rules or by order of court for doing any act required or allowed under these rules, or may permit an act to be done after the expiration of such time. Courts may not extend the time for taking an appeal or for filing a petition for discretionary review or a petition for rehearing or the responses thereto prescribed by these rules or by law.

(1) Motions for Extension of Time in the Trial Division. The trial tribunal for good cause shown by the appellant may extend once for no more than thirty days the time permitted by Rule 11 or Rule 18 for service of the proposed record on appeal.

Motions for extensions of time made to a trial tribunal may be made orally or in writing and without notice to other parties and may be determined at any time or place within the state.

Motions made under this Rule 27 to a court of the trial division may be heard and determined by any of those judges of the particular court specified in Rule 36 of these rules. Such motions made to a commission may be heard and

---

44   *State ex rel. Thornburg v. Currency*, 324 N.C. 276, 378 S.E.2d 1 (1989).

determined by the chair of the commission; or if to a commissioner, then by that commissioner.

(2) Motions for Extension of Time in the Appellate Division. All motions for extensions of time other than those specifically enumerated in Rule 27(c)(1) may be made only to the appellate court to which appeal has been taken.

(d) Motions for Extension of Time; How Determined. Motions for extension of time made in any court may be determined ex parte, but the moving party shall promptly serve on all other parties to the appeal a copy of any order extending time; provided that motions made after the expiration of the time allowed in these rules for the action sought to be extended must be in writing and with notice to all other parties and may be allowed only after all other parties have had an opportunity to be heard.

CHAPTER TWELVE: MOTIONS AND BRIEFS

RULE 28: Briefs; Function and Content.

Rule 28(a) describes the function of Rule 28 as a whole as it pertains to briefs. The parties submit briefs to clearly outline the issues and arguments to the court. The court limits its review to the issues presented in the briefs. Note that Rule 28(a) states that "Questions raised by assignments of error in appeals from trial tribunals but not then presented and discussed in a party's brief, are deemed abandoned." In *Jones v. City of Durham*, 361 N.C. 144, 638 S.E.2d 202 (2006), the plaintiff, who raised two issues in her notice of appeal based on a dissenting opinion in the Court of Appeals, abandoned her appeal as of right as to a obstruction of justice issue, where the brief addressed only whether summary judgment was properly granted as to the gross negligence claim. Frequently, the appellant lists numerous assignments of error in the record, but only briefs a few. A diligent Appellee will note in his/her brief that any issues raised in the assignments of error but not discussed in the brief are deemed abandoned.

Rule 28(b) is self-explanatory. These are the items that must be present in each appellant brief. These items should be set out using a heading. The items include: (1) a cover page; (2) index page; (3) table of authorities; (4) listing of the issues; (5) statement of the case detailing the procedural history of the case up until the appeal; (6) statement of grounds for appellate review; (7) statement of the facts; (8) arguments; (9) conclusion stating the precise relief sought by appellant; (10) counsel identifications (including signature, typed name, address and telephone number); (11) certificate of service; and (12) an appendix, if any. Upon receiving the appellant's brief, look closely to make sure all of these items are included. If anything is missing, immediately file a motion to dismiss based upon Rule 28(b). However, do not wait for the court to rule on your motion to begin your brief.

Rule 28(c) states the necessary content of the appellee's brief. The items are the same as the appellant's brief except for statement of issues, statement of the procedural history of the case, statement of the grounds for appellate review, statement of the facts, or statement of the standard(s) of review. However, the Appellee brief may include a restatement of any of these items if the appellee disagrees with the appellant's statements. The Appellee brief must also include: (1) a subject index; (2) table of authorities; (3) argument; (4) specific conclusion; (5) identification of counsel; and (6) proof of service. An appendix, if any, should be attached to the brief. If the Appellee desires to bring cross-assignments of error, they should be included as well, even if the Appellee did not appeal or make cross-assignments of error. However, these cross assignments of error may only include whether a new trial should be granted to the appellee rather than a judgment n.o.v. awarded to the appellant as long as the latter relief is sought on appeal by the appellant.

Rule 28(d) speaks only to appendices and explains when they should be attached to briefs. When a transcript is filed under Rule 9(c)(2), the parties must file verbatim portions of the transcript as appendices to their briefs, if required by this Rule 29(d). Appendices to an appellant's brief are required when: (1) it is necessary to understand any issue presented in the brief; (2) when discussing an exchange occurring during a hearing regarding the admission of evidence; (3) relevant portions of a statute rule or regulation are needed to determine the issue; (4) items pursuant to Rules 11(c) or 8(d)(3). An appellee must include an appendix when: (1) the appellee believes the appellant omitted something important in its appendix; or (2) the appellee brings forth a new or additional issue. Rule 26(g) summarizes the format of appendices.

Rule 28(e) requires that references to assignments of error be by their numbers as listed in the record. Rule 28(f) allows parties to join their arguments in a single brief even if they are not formally joined in the appeal. Any party is allowed to adopt portions of another party's brief(s) by reference.

Under Rule 28(g), a party can file a memorandum of additional authority after the brief has already been filed. This memo can be filed to bring the court's attention to a case that has been decided after the brief was filed but before the court has heard the case. When filing the memo to the Court of Appeals, there should be an original and 3 copies. When filing it at the Supreme Court, there should be an original and 14 copies.

Pursuant to Rule 28(h), an appellant can file a reply brief if the appellee presented new issues in its brief or if the case will not be heard orally. All reply briefs must be filed within 14 days of the appellee's brief filing date. ** Note: Motions for extensions of time to file a reply brief are disfavored.

Rule 28(i) describes when and how an amicus brief may be filed. An amicus curiae must file a motion to the appellate court asking for permission to file an amicus brief. The motion must state the following: (1) the nature of the applicant's interest; (2) the reasons why the brief is believed desirable; (3) the issues to be addressed; and (4) the position of the amicus on those issues. Generally, the amicus brief is due at the same time as the appellant's brief and there is no oral argument. An amicus cannot file a reply brief.

Rule 28(j) explains the page limits and formatting of the briefs. All parties must use Courier or Courier New 12-point font or Times New Roman 14-point font. Courier/Courier New briefs have a 35-page limit. Reply briefs have a 15-page limit and amicus briefs are limited to 15 pages. Cover pages, index pages, tables of authority pages, certificates of service and appendices are not counted in the page limit. Times New Roman briefs cannot have more 8,750 words. Reply and amicus briefs can only have 3,750 words. Rule 28(j) requires parties using Times New Roman font to include a certification page just before the certificate of service page stating the number of words used in the brief, including footnotes and citations. The certification page must be signed by counsel and state that the brief "contains no more than the number of words allowed by Rule 28(j)."

(a) Function. The function of all briefs required or permitted by these rules is to define clearly the issues presented to the reviewing court and to present the arguments and authorities upon which the parties rely in support of their respective positions thereon. The scope of review on appeal is limited to issues so presented in the several briefs. Issues not presented and discussed in a party's brief are deemed abandoned. Similarly, issues properly presented for review in the Court of Appeals, but not then stated in the notice of appeal or the petition accepted by the Supreme Court for review and discussed in the new briefs required by Rules 14(d)(1) and 15(g)(2) to be filed in the Supreme Court for review by that Court, are deemed abandoned.

Parties shall protect the identity of juveniles covered by Rules 3(b)(1), 3.1(b), or 4(e) pursuant to said rules.

(b) Content of Appellant's Brief. An appellant's brief shall contain, under appropriate headings and in the form prescribed by Rule 26(g) and the appendixes to these rules, in the following order:

(1) A cover page, followed by a subject index and table of authorities as required by Rule 26(g).

(2) A statement of the issues presented for review. The proposed issues on appeal listed in the record on appeal shall not limit the scope of the issues that an appellant may argue in its brief.

(3) A concise statement of the procedural history of the case. This shall indicate the nature of the case and summarize the course of proceedings up to the taking of the appeal before the court.

(4) A statement of the grounds for appellate review. Such statement shall include citation of the statute or statutes permitting appellate review. When an appeal is based on Rule 54(b) of the Rules of Civil Procedure, the statement shall show that there has been a final judgment as to one or more but fewer than all of the claims or parties and that there has been a certification by the trial court that there is no just reason for delay. When an appeal is interlocutory, the statement must contain sufficient facts and argument to support appellate review on the ground that the challenged order affects a substantial right.

(5) A full and complete statement of the facts. This should be a non-argumentative summary of all material facts underlying the matter in controversy which are necessary to understand all issues presented for review, supported by references to pages in the transcript of proceedings, the record on appeal, or exhibits, as the case may be.

(6) An argument, to contain the contentions of the appellant with respect to each issue presented. Issues not presented in a party's brief, or in support of which no reason or argument is stated, will be taken as abandoned.

The argument shall contain a concise statement of the applicable standard(s) of review for each issue, which shall appear either at the beginning of the discussion of each issue or under a separate heading placed before the beginning of the discussion of all the issues.

The body of the argument and the statement of applicable standard(s) of review shall contain citations of the authorities upon which the appellant relies. Evidence or other proceedings material to the issue may be narrated or quoted in the body of the argument, with appropriate reference to the record on appeal, the transcript of proceedings, or exhibits.

(7) A short conclusion stating the precise relief sought.

(8) Identification of counsel by signature, typed name, post office address, telephone number, State Bar number, and e-mail address.

(9) The proof of service required by Rule 26(d).

(10) Any appendix required or allowed by this Rule 28.

(c) Content of Appellee's Brief; Presentation of Additional Issues. An appellee's brief shall contain a subject index and table of authorities as required by Rule 26(g), an argument, a conclusion, identification of counsel, and proof of service in the form provided in Rule 28(b) for an appellant's brief, and any appendix required or allowed by this Rule 28. It need contain no statement of the issues presented, of the procedural history of the case, of the grounds for appellate review, of the facts, or of the standard(s) of review, unless the appellee disagrees with the appellant's statements and desires to make a restatement or unless the appellee desires to present issues in addition to those stated by the appellant.

Without taking an appeal, an appellee may present issues on appeal based on any action or omission of the trial court that deprived the appellee of an alternative basis in law for supporting the judgment, order, or other determination from which appeal has been taken. Without having taken appeal or listing proposed issues as permitted by Rule 10(c), an appellee may also argue on appeal whether a new trial should be granted to the appellee rather than a judgment notwithstanding the verdict awarded to the appellant when the latter relief is sought on appeal by the appellant. If the appellee presents issues in addition to those stated by the appellant, the appellee's brief must contain a full, non-argumentative summary of all material facts necessary to understand the new issues supported by references to pages in the record on appeal, the transcript of proceedings, or the appendixes, as appropriate, as well as a statement of the applicable standard(s) of review for those additional issues.

An appellee may supplement the record with any materials pertinent to the issues presented on appeal, as provided in Rule 9(b)(5).

(d) Appendixes to Briefs. Whenever the transcript of proceedings is filed pursuant to Rule 9(c)(2), the parties must file verbatim portions of the transcript as appendixes to their briefs, if required by this Rule 28(d). Parties must modify verbatim portions of the transcript filed pursuant to this rule in a manner consistent with Rules 3(b)(1), 3.1(b), or 4(e).

(1) When Appendixes to Appellant's Brief Are Required. Except as provided in Rule 28(d)(2), the appellant must reproduce as appendixes to its brief:

a. those portions of the transcript of proceedings which must be reproduced verbatim in order to understand any issue presented in the brief;

b. those portions of the transcript showing the pertinent questions and answers when an issue presented in the brief involves the admission or exclusion of evidence;

c. relevant portions of statutes, rules, or regulations, the study of which is required to determine issues presented in the brief;

d. relevant items from the Rule 11(c) or Rule 18(d)(3) supplement to the printed record on appeal, the study of which are required to determine issues presented in the brief.

(2) When Appendixes to Appellant's Brief Are Not Required. Notwithstanding the requirements of Rule 28(d)(1), the appellant is not required to reproduce an appendix to its brief with respect to an issue presented:

a. whenever the portion of the transcript necessary to understand an issue presented in the brief is reproduced verbatim in the body of the brief;

b. to show the absence or insufficiency of evidence unless there are discrete portions of the transcript where the subject matter of the alleged insufficiency of the evidence is located; or

c. to show the general nature of the evidence necessary to understand an issue presented in the brief if such evidence has been fully summarized as required by Rule 28(b)(4) and (5).

(3) When Appendixes to Appellee's Brief Are Required. An appellee must reproduce appendixes to its brief in the following circumstances:

a. Whenever the appellee believes that appellant's appendixes do not include portions of the transcript or items from the Rule 11(c) or Rule 18(d)(3) supplement to the printed record on appeal that are required by Rule 28(d)(1), the appellee shall reproduce those portions of the transcript or supplement it believes to be necessary to understand the issue.

b. Whenever the appellee presents a new or additional issue in its brief as permitted by Rule 28(c), the appellee shall reproduce portions of the transcript or relevant items from the Rule 11(c) or Rule 18(d)(3) supplement to the printed record on appeal as if it were the appellant with respect to each such new or additional issue.

(4) Format of Appendixes. The appendixes to the briefs of any party shall be in the format prescribed by Rule 26(g) and shall consist of clear photocopies of transcript pages that have been deemed necessary for inclusion in the appendix under this Rule 28(d). The pages of the appendix shall be consecutively numbered, and an index to the appendix shall be placed at its beginning.

(e) References in Briefs to the Record. References in the briefs to parts of the printed record on appeal and to parts of the verbatim transcript or parts of documentary exhibits shall be to the pages where those portions appear.

(f) Joinder of Multiple Parties in Briefs. Any number of appellants or appellees in a single cause or in causes consolidated for appeal may join in a single brief even though they are not formally joined on the appeal. Any party to any appeal may adopt by reference portions of the briefs of others.

(g) Additional Authorities. Additional authorities discovered by a party after filing its brief may be brought to the attention of the court by filing a memorandum thereof with the clerk of the court and serving copies upon all other parties. The memorandum may not be used as a reply brief or for additional argument, but shall simply state the issue to which the additional authority applies and provide a full citation of the authority. Authorities not cited in the briefs or in such a memorandum may not be cited and discussed in oral argument.

Before the Court of Appeals, the party shall file an original and three copies of the memorandum; in the Supreme Court, the party shall file an original and fourteen copies of the memorandum.

(h) Reply Briefs. No reply brief will be received or considered by the court, except in the following circumstances:
(1) The court, upon its own initiative, may order a reply brief to be filed and served.

(2) If the appellee has presented in its brief new or additional issues as permitted by Rule 28(c), an appellant may, within fourteen days after service of such brief, file and serve a reply brief limited to those new or additional issues.

(3) If the parties are notified under Rule 30(f) that the case will be submitted without oral argument on the record and briefs, an appellant may, within fourteen days after service of such notification, file and serve a reply brief limited to a concise rebuttal to arguments set out in the brief of the appellee which were not addressed in the appellant's principal brief or in a reply brief filed pursuant to Rule 28(h)(1).

(4) If the parties are notified that the case has been scheduled for oral argument, an appellant may, within fourteen days after service of such notification, file and serve a motion for leave to file a reply brief. The motion shall state concisely the reasons why a reply brief is believed to be desirable or necessary and the issues to be addressed in the reply brief. The proposed reply brief may be submitted with the motion for leave and shall be limited to a concise rebuttal to arguments set out in the brief of the appellee which were not addressed in the appellant's principal brief. Unless otherwise ordered by the court, the motion for leave will be determined solely upon the motion and without responses thereto or oral argument. The clerk of the appellate court will notify the parties of the court's action upon the motion, and, if the motion is granted, the appellant shall file and serve the reply brief within ten days of such notice.

(5) Motions for extensions of time in relation to reply briefs are disfavored.

(i) Amicus Curiae Briefs. A brief of an amicus curiae may be filed only by leave of the appellate court wherein the appeal is docketed or in response to a request made by that court on its own initiative.

A person desiring to file an amicus curiae brief shall present to the court a motion for leave to file, served upon all parties. The motion shall state concisely the nature of the applicant's interest, the reasons why an amicus curiae brief is believed desirable, the issues of law to be addressed in the amicus curiae brief, and the applicant's position on those issues. The proposed amicus curiae brief may be conditionally filed with the motion for leave. Unless otherwise ordered by the court, the application for leave will be determined solely upon the motion and without responses thereto or oral argument.

The clerk of the appellate court will forthwith notify the applicant and all parties of the court's action upon the application. Unless other time limits are set out in the order of the court permitting the brief, the amicus curiae shall file the brief within the time allowed for the filing of the brief of the party supported or, if in support of neither party, within the time allowed for filing appellant's brief. Motions for leave to file an amicus curiae brief submitted to the court after the time within which the amicus curiae brief normally would be due are disfavored in the absence of good cause. Reply briefs of the parties to an amicus curiae brief will be limited to points or authorities presented in the amicus curiae brief which are not presented in the main briefs of the parties. No reply brief of an amicus curiae will be received.

A motion of an amicus curiae to participate in oral argument will be allowed only for extraordinary reasons.

(j) Length Limitations Applicable to Briefs Filed in the Court of Appeals. Each brief filed in the Court of Appeals, whether filed by an appellant, appellee, or amicus curiae, formatted according to Rule 26 and the appendixes to these rules, shall have either a page limit or a word-count limit, depending on the type style used in the brief:

(1) Type.

(A) Type style. Documents must be set in a plain roman style, although italics or boldface may be used for emphasis. Case names must be italicized or underlined. Documents may be set in either proportionally spaced or nonproportionally spaced (monospaced) type.

(B) Type size.

1. Nonproportionally spaced type (e.g., Courier or Courier New) may not contain more than ten characters per inch (12-point).

2. Proportionally spaced type (e.g., Times New Roman) must be 14-point or larger.

3. Documents set in Courier New 12-point type or Times New Roman 14-point type will be deemed in compliance with these type size requirements.

(2) Document.

(A) Page limits for briefs using nonproportional type. The page limit for a principal brief that uses nonproportional type is thirty-five pages. The page limit for a reply brief permitted by Rule 28(h)(1), (2), or (3) is fifteen pages, and the page limit for a reply brief permitted by Rule 28(h)(4) is twelve pages. Unless otherwise ordered by the court, the page limit for an amicus curiae brief is fifteen pages. A page shall contain no more than twenty-seven lines of double-spaced text of no more than sixty-five characters per line. Covers, indexes, tables of authorities, certificates of service, and appendixes do not count toward these page limits. The court may strike or require resubmission of briefs with excessive single-spaced passages or footnotes that are used to circumvent these page limits.

(B) Word-count limits for briefs using proportional type. A principal brief that uses proportional type may contain no more than 8,750 words. A reply brief permitted by Rule 28(h)(1), (2), or (3) may contain no more than 3,750 words, and a reply brief permitted by Rule 28(h)(4) may contain no more than 3,000 words. Unless otherwise ordered by the court, an amicus curiae brief may contain no more than 3,750 words. Covers, indexes, tables of authorities, certificates of service, certificates of compliance with this rule, and appendixes do not count against these word-count limits. Footnotes and citations in the text, however, do count against these word-count limits. Parties who file briefs in proportional type shall submit with the brief, immediately before the certificate of service, a certification, signed by counsel of record, or in the case of parties filing briefs pro se, by the party, that the brief contains no more than the number of words allowed by this rule. For purposes of this certification, counsel and parties may rely on word counts reported by word-processing software, as long as footnotes and citations are included in those word counts.

RULE 29: Sessions of Courts; Calendar of Hearings.

Rule 29(a) states that the Supreme Court will hold oral arguments of appeals in every month except June, July and August, although additional court days can be set by the chief justice. The Court of Appeals is always in continuous session and the panels will be assigned by the chief judge.

Rule 29(b) provides that cases will be heard on a first-file, first-heard basis, unless the court determines otherwise. Parties can move the court to have priority calendaring.

(a) Sessions of Court.

(1) Supreme Court. The Supreme Court shall be in continuous session for the transaction of business. Unless otherwise scheduled by the Court, hearings in appeals will be held during the months of February through May and September through December. Additional settings may be authorized by the Chief Justice.

(2) Court of Appeals. Appeals will be heard in accordance with a schedule promulgated by the Chief Judge. Panels of the Court will sit as scheduled by the Chief Judge. For the transaction of other business, the Court of Appeals shall be in continuous session.

(b) Calendaring of Cases for Hearing. Each appellate court will calendar the hearing of all appeals docketed in the court. In general, appeals will be calendared for hearing in the order in which they are docketed, but the court may vary the order for any cause deemed appropriate. On motion of any party, with notice to all other parties, the court may determine without hearing to give an appeal peremptory setting or otherwise to vary the normal calendar order. Except as advanced for peremptory setting on motion of a party or the court's own initiative, no appeal will be calendared for hearing at a time less than thirty days after the filing of the appellant's brief. The clerk of the appellate court will give reasonable notice to all counsel of record of the setting of an appeal for hearing by mailing a copy of the calendar.

RULE 30: Oral Argument and Unpublished Opinions.

Rule 30(a) provides the format of oral arguments before both appellate courts. The appellant goes first and is allowed to reserve part of his/her time for rebuttal. The parties are not allowed to read from their briefs. The appellant's opening argument should include a refresher on the facts. **Counsel may not use a juvenile's name.

Rule 30(b) gives both parties 30 minutes total for oral argument. Thus, if the appellant wishes a rebuttal, the appellant must request it before beginning. Counsel does not have to use all of the 30 minutes and may move the court, prior to oral argument, for more time.

Rule 30(c) allows the court to hear only one side of the argument if one of the parties does not appear. If neither party appears, the court will decide the issues on the briefs only. Rule 30(d) allows parties to agree to have a case decided solely on the briefs. However, the court can always order oral argument.

Rule 30(e) states that the Court of Appeals is not required to publish an opinion in every case it hears. Due to cost concerns, the panel will determine whether an opinion should be published. Non-published cases do not constitute controlling legal authority. Therefore, they should not be cited unless there is not a published case that would serve as well. If a party cites an unpublished case, a copy of the case should be attached to the brief. Parties can move for the publication of an unpublished opinion within 10 days of its filing. Rule 30(f) allows for both appellate courts to dispose of a case without oral arguments. See Appendix C for tips regarding oral arguments.

(a) Order and Content of Argument.

(1) The appellant is entitled to open and conclude the argument. The opening argument shall include a fair statement of the case. Oral arguments should complement the written briefs, and counsel will therefore not be permitted to read at length from briefs, records, and authorities.

(2) In cases involving juveniles covered by Rules 3(b)(1), 3.1(b), or 4(e), counsel shall refrain from using a juvenile's name in oral argument and shall refer to the juvenile pursuant to said rules.

(b) Time Allowed for Argument.

(1) In General. Ordinarily a total of thirty minutes will be allowed all appellants and a total of thirty minutes will be allowed all appellees for oral argument. Upon written or oral application of any party, the court for good cause shown may extend the times limited for argument. Among other causes, the existence of adverse interests between multiple appellants or between multiple appellees may be suggested as good cause for such an extension. The court of its own initiative may direct argument on specific points outside the times limited.

Counsel is not obliged to use all the time allowed, and should avoid unnecessary repetition; the court may terminate argument whenever it considers further argument unnecessary.

(2) Numerous Counsel. Any number of counsel representing individual appellants or appellees proceeding separately or jointly may be heard in argument within the times herein limited or allowed by order of court. When more than one counsel is heard, duplication or supplementation of argument on the same points shall be avoided unless specifically directed by the court.

(c) Non-Appearance of Parties. If counsel for any party fails to appear to present oral argument, the court will hear argument from opposing counsel. If counsel for no party appears, the court will decide the case on the written briefs unless it orders otherwise.

(d) Submission on Written Briefs. By agreement of the parties, a case may be submitted for decision on the written briefs, but the court may nevertheless order oral argument before deciding the case.

(e) Unpublished Opinions.

(1) In order to minimize the cost of publication and of providing storage space for the published reports, the Court of Appeals is not required to publish an opinion in every decided case. If the panel that hears the case determines that the appeal involves no new legal principles and that an opinion, if published, would have no value as a precedent, it may direct that no opinion be published.

(2) The text of a decision without published opinion shall be posted on the Administrative Office of the Courts' North Carolina Court System Internet web site and reported only by listing the case and the decision in the advance sheets and the bound volumes of the North Carolina Court of Appeals Reports.

(3) An unpublished decision of the North Carolina Court of Appeals does not constitute controlling legal authority. Accordingly, citation of unpublished opinions in briefs, memoranda, and oral arguments in the trial and appellate divisions is disfavored, except for the purpose of establishing claim preclusion, issue preclusion, or the law of the case. If a party believes, nevertheless, that an unpublished opinion has precedential value to a material issue in the case and that there is no published opinion that would serve as well, the party may cite the unpublished opinion if that party serves a copy thereof on all other parties in the case and on the court to which the citation is offered. This service may be accomplished by including the copy of the unpublished opinion in an addendum to a brief or memorandum. A party who cites an unpublished

opinion for the first time at a hearing or oral argument must attach a copy of the unpublished opinion relied upon pursuant to the requirements of Rule 28(g). When citing an unpublished opinion, a party must indicate the opinion's unpublished status.

(4) Counsel of record and pro se parties of record may move for publication of an unpublished opinion, citing reasons based on Rule 30(e)(1) and serving a copy of the motion upon all other counsel and pro se parties of record. The motion shall be filed and served within ten days of the filing of the opinion. Any objection to the requested publication by counsel or pro se parties of record must be filed within five days after service of the motion requesting publication. The panel that heard the case shall determine whether to allow or deny such motion.

(f) Pre-Argument Review; Decision of Appeal Without Oral Argument.

(1) At any time that the Supreme Court concludes that oral argument in any case pending before it will not be of assistance to the Court, it may dispose of the case on the record and briefs. In those cases, counsel will be notified not to appear for oral argument.

(2) The Chief Judge of the Court of Appeals may from time to time designate a panel to review any pending case, after all briefs are filed but before argument, for decision under this rule. If all of the judges of the panel to which a pending appeal has been referred conclude that oral argument will not be of assistance to the Court, the case may be disposed of on the record and briefs. Counsel will be notified not to appear for oral argument.

RULE 31: Petition for Rehearing.

According to Rule 31(a), a party can petition for a rehearing 15 days after the mandate of the appellate court. The petitioning party must state specifically the points of fact or law that the court has misapprehended or overlooked. The petition must include a certificate from at least two disinterested attorneys.

Rule 31(b) states that the petition must be addressed to the court which heard issued the opinion. Rule 31(c) gives the court 30 days to accept or deny the petition. This decision is final.

Under Rule 31(d), if the petition is granted, the court will use only the record on appeal, petition, new briefs and oral argument, if any. The petitioner's new brief is due 30 days after the petition is granted. The other party's brief is due 30 days after the petitioner's brief is served. Rule 31(e) allows the petitioner to move for a stay of execution pursuant to Rule 8. Under Rule 31(f), if the losing party files a notice of appeal to the Supreme Court, no petition will be entertained by the Court of Appeals. Under Rule 31(g), there are no petitions for rehearing in criminal cases.

(a) Time for Filing; Content. A petition for rehearing may be filed in a civil action within fifteen days after the mandate of the court has been issued. The petition shall state with particularity the points of fact or law that, in the opinion of the petitioner, the court has overlooked or misapprehended and shall contain such argument in support of the petition as petitioner desires to present. It shall be accompanied by a certificate of at least two attorneys who for periods of at least five years, respectively, shall have been members of the bar of this State and who have no interest in the subject of the action and have not been counsel for any party to the action, that they have carefully examined the appeal and the authorities cited in the decision, and that they consider the decision in error on points specifically and concisely identified. Oral argument in support of the petition will not be permitted.

(b) How Addressed; Filed. A petition for rehearing shall be addressed to the court that issued the opinion sought to be reconsidered.

(c) How Determined. Within thirty days after the petition is filed, the court will either grant or deny the petition. A determination to grant or deny will be made solely upon the written petition; no written response will be received from the opposing party and no oral argument by any party will be heard. Determination by the court is final. The rehearing may be granted as to all or fewer than all points suggested in the petition. When the petition is denied, the clerk shall forthwith notify all parties.

(d) Procedure When Granted. Upon grant of the petition the clerk shall forthwith notify the parties that the petition has been granted. The case will be reconsidered solely upon the record on appeal, the petition to rehear, new briefs of both parties, and the oral argument if one has been ordered by the court. The briefs shall be addressed solely to the points specified in the order granting the petition to rehear. The petitioner's brief shall be filed within thirty days after the case is certified for rehearing, and the opposing party's brief, within thirty days after petitioner's brief is served. Filing and service of the new briefs shall be in accordance with the requirements of Rule 13. No reply brief shall be received on rehearing. If the court has ordered oral argument, the clerk shall give notice of the time set therefor, which time shall be not less than thirty days after the filing of the petitioner's brief on rehearing.

(e) Stay of Execution. When a petition for rehearing is filed, the petitioner may obtain a stay of execution in the trial court to which the mandate of the appellate court has been issued. The procedure is as provided by Rule 8 of these rules for stays pending appeal.

(f) Waiver by Appeal from Court of Appeals. The timely filing of a notice of appeal from, or of a petition for discretionary review of, a determination of the Court of Appeals constitutes a waiver of any right thereafter to petition the Court of Appeals for rehearing as to such determination or, if a petition for rehearing has earlier been filed, an abandonment of such petition.

(g) No Petition in Criminal Cases. The courts will not entertain petitions for rehearing in criminal actions.

RULE 37: Motions in Appellate Courts (taken out of order).

Rule 37 governs motions made in the appellate courts. Pursuant to Rule 37(a), a motion may be filed at any time before the case is called for oral argument. The non-movant has 10 days to respond to the motion. The court may act upon a motion at any time. In *Warren v. Warren*, 175 N.C. App. 509, 623 S.E.2d 800 (2006), our Court of Appeals was not required to address a wife's motion to dismiss her husband's appeal in a divorce action, even though she included it in the opening pages of her appellate brief, because the motion was not filed in accordance with this rule.

Under Rule 37(c), a motion may not contain the name of a juvenile. Under Rule 37(d), the court will not listen to oral arguments regarding motions, although a party may ask for reconsideration.

Rule 37(e) details how an appellant can withdraw an appeal. The appellant does not need the consent of the other party(ies) and can simply file a notice of withdrawal before the record has been docketed. After the record has been docketed, the appellant, with or without other parties, must move to withdraw an appeal. Rule 37(f) states that any withdrawal will not affect another party's rights of appeal or to continue the instant appeal. See Appendix A for more information on writing appellate motions.

(a) Time; Content of Motions; Response. An application to a court of the appellate division for an order or for other relief available under these rules may be made by filing a motion for such order or other relief with the clerk of the court, with service on all other parties. Unless another time is expressly provided by these rules, the motion may be filed and served at any time before the case is called for oral argument. The motion shall contain or be accompanied by any matter required by a specific provision of these rules governing such a motion and shall state with particularity the grounds on which it is based and the order or relief sought. If a motion is supported by affidavits, briefs, or other papers, these shall be served and filed with the motion. Within ten days after a motion is served or until the appeal is called for oral argument, whichever period is shorter, a party may file and serve copies of a response in opposition to the motion, which may be supported by affidavits, briefs, or other papers in the same manner as motions. The court may shorten or extend the time for responding to any motion.

(b) Determination. Notwithstanding the provisions of Rule 37(a), a motion may be acted upon at any time, despite the absence of notice to all parties and without awaiting a response thereto. A party who has not received actual notice of such a motion, or who has not filed a response at the time such action is taken, and who is adversely affected by the action may request reconsideration, vacation, or modification thereof. Motions will be determined without argument, unless the court orders otherwise.

(c) Protecting the Identity of Certain Juveniles. Parties shall protect the identity of juveniles covered by Rules 3(b)(1), 3.1(b), or 4(e) pursuant to said rules.

(d) Withdrawal of Appeal in Criminal Cases. Withdrawal of appeal in criminal cases shall be in accordance with N.C.G.S. § 15A-1450. In addition to the requirements of N.C.G.S. § 15A-1450, after the record on appeal in a criminal case has been filed in an appellate court but before the filing of an opinion, the defendant shall also file a written notice of the withdrawal with the clerk of the appropriate appellate court.

(e) Withdrawal of Appeal in Civil Cases.

(1) Prior to the filing of a record on appeal in the appellate court, an appellant or cross-appellant may, without the consent of the other party, file a notice of withdrawal of its appeal with the tribunal from which appeal has been taken. Alternatively, prior to the filing of a record on appeal, the parties may file a signed stipulation agreeing to dismiss the appeal with the tribunal from which the appeal has been taken.

(2) After the record on appeal has been filed, an appellant or cross-appellant or all parties jointly may move the appellate court in which the appeal is pending, prior to the filing of an opinion, for dismissal of the appeal. The motion must specify the reasons therefor, the positions of all parties on the motion to dismiss, and the positions of all parties on the allocation of taxed costs. The appeal may be dismissed by order upon such terms as agreed to by the parties or as fixed by the appellate court.

(f) Effect of Withdrawal of Appeal. The withdrawal of an appeal shall not affect the right of any other party to file or continue such party's appeal or cross-appeal.

CHAPTER THIRTEEN: MISCELLANEOUS ATTORNEY RULES

RULE 6: Costs (taken out of order).

Rule 6 outlines the procedure for handling security for costs on appeal. This rule applies to GAL cases in which GAL is the appellant. Under N.C.G.S. 7B-2000, all juveniles are presumed indigent. So, if you are filing an appeal on GAL's behalf, you are exempt from the Rule 6(a) security requirement. It is interesting to note that this statute is found in the juvenile delinquency code and not the 7B subchapter that deals with abused, neglected and dependent children. Both subchapters were part of the same legislation at one time (the Juvenile Code), which most likely explains the statute's location.

(a) In Regular Course. Except in pauper appeals, an appellant in a civil action must provide adequate security for the costs of appeal in accordance with the provisions of N.C.G.S. §§ 1-285 and -286.

(b) In Forma Pauperis Appeals. A party in a civil action may be allowed to prosecute an appeal in forma pauperis without providing security for costs in accordance with the provisions of N.C.G.S. § 1-288.

(c) Filed with Record on Appeal. When security for costs is required, the appellant shall file with the record on appeal a certified copy of the appeal bond or a cash deposit made in lieu of bond.

(d) Dismissal for Failure to File or Defect in Security. For failure of the appellant to provide security as required by subsection (a) or to file evidence thereof as required by subsection (c), or for a substantial defect or irregularity in any security provided, the appeal may on motion of an appellee be dismissed by the appellate court where docketed, unless for good cause shown the court permits the security to be provided or the filing to be made out of time, or the defect or irregularity to be corrected. A motion to dismiss on these grounds shall be made and determined in accordance with Rule 37. When the motion to dismiss is made on the grounds of a defect or irregularity, the appellant may as a matter of right correct the defect or irregularity by filing a proper bond or making proper deposit with the clerk of the appellate court within ten days after service of the motion upon appellant or before the case is called for argument, whichever first occurs.

(e) No Security for Costs in Criminal Appeals. Pursuant to N.C.G.S. § 15A-1449, no security for costs is required upon appeal of criminal cases to the appellate division.

RULE 32: Mandates of the Courts.

Rule 32 provides that a mandate from an opinion is not issued until 20 days after it is filed with the clerk.

(a) In General. Unless a court of the appellate division directs that a formal mandate shall issue, the mandate of the court consists of certified copies of its judgment and of its opinion and any direction of its clerk as to costs. The mandate is issued by its transmittal from the clerk of the issuing court to the clerk or comparable officer of the tribunal from which appeal was taken to the issuing court.

(b) Time of Issuance. Unless a court orders otherwise, its clerk shall enter judgment and issue the mandate of the court twenty days after the written opinion of the court has been filed with the clerk.

RULE 33: Attorneys.

Rule 33(a) states that an attorney is not recognized unless he/she is entered on the record as counsel. A signature on any document filed with the court will constitute entry of the counsel of record. Upon accepting an appeal, an attorney should file a Notice of Appearance with the appellate Court and serve all parties, including the transcriptionist if the transcript has not yet been served. Counsel of record may not withdraw from a case except by leave of court. Only counsel who have personally signed the brief prior to oral argument may be heard in argument. Practice Tip: If you plan on arguing during oral arguments and you are not sure whether you personally signed the brief, arrive a few minutes early and check the original brief in the clerk's office. If your signature is not there, sign the brief at that time and inform the judges/justices that you have done so at the oral argument.

Pursuant to Rule 33(b), the attorney who electronically files a document must list his/her name first and if there are other names, certify that all of the other listed attorneys have authorized him/her to list their names as if they had personally signed the document themselves. Rule 33(c) allows the courts to only recognize attorney agreements filed in the record on appeal or filed after the appeal has been docketed.

Note the changes made regarding out-of-state attorneys. They now have to submit a motion prior to or at the same time with the filing of the motion, brief, etc. Additionally, the attorney will have to file a separate motion in the Supreme Court even if the Court of Appeals has allowed her to appear before it.

(a) Appearances. An attorney will not be recognized as appearing in any case unless he or she is entered as counsel of record therein. The signature of an attorney on a record on appeal, motion, brief, or other document permitted by these rules to be filed in a court of the appellate division constitutes entry of the attorney as counsel of record for the parties designated and a certification that the attorney represents such parties. The signature of a member or associate in a firm's name constitutes entry of the firm as counsel of record for the parties designated. Counsel of record may not withdraw from a case except by leave of court. Only those counsel of record who have personally signed the brief prior to oral argument may be heard in argument.

(b) Signatures on Electronically Filed Documents. If more than one attorney is listed as being an attorney for the party(ies) on an electronically filed document, it is the responsibility of the attorney actually filing the document by computer to (1) list his or her name first on the document, and (2) place on the document under the signature line the following statement: "I certify that all of the attorneys listed below have authorized me to list their names on this document as if they had personally signed it."

(c) Agreements. Only those agreements of counsel which appear in the record on appeal or which are filed in the court where an appeal is docketed will be recognized by that court.

(d) Limited Practice of Out-of-State Attorneys. Attorneys who are not licensed to practice law in North Carolina, but desire to appear before the appellate courts of North Carolina in a matter shall submit a motion to the appellate court fully complying with the requirements set forth in N.C.G. S. § 84-4.1. This motion shall be filed prior to or contemporaneously with the out-of-state attorney signing and filing any motion, petition, brief, or other document in any appellate court. Failure to comply with this provision may subject the attorney to sanctions and shall result in the document being stricken, unless signed by another attorney licensed to practice in North Carolina. If an attorney is admitted to practice before the Court of Appeals in a matter, the attorney shall be required to file another motion should the case proceed to the Supreme Court. However, if the required fee has been paid to the Court of Appeals, another fee shall not be due at the Supreme Court.

RULE 33.1: Secure Leave Periods for Attorneys.

Under Rule 33.1, counsel may secure leave. The leave period is divided into weeks and cannot exceed 3 aggregate weeks. In order to designate leave, an attorney must file a designation to the appellate clerk's office at least 90 days before the leave period and before any argument has been scheduled in the case. The designation must include certain information as listed in Rule 33.1(D).

(a) Purpose, Authorization. In order to secure for the parties to actions and proceedings pending in the appellate division, and to the public at large, the heightened level of professionalism that an attorney is able to provide when the attorney enjoys periods of time that are free from the urgent demands of professional responsibility and to enhance the overall quality of the attorney's personal and family life, any attorney may from time to time designate and enjoy one or more secure leave periods each year as provided in this rule.

(b) Length, Number. A secure leave period shall consist of one or more complete calendar weeks. During any calendar year, an attorney's secure leave periods pursuant to this rule and to Rule 26 of the General Rules of Practice for the Superior and District Courts shall not exceed, in the aggregate, three calendar weeks.

(c) Designation, Effect. To designate a secure leave period, an attorney shall file a written designation containing the information required by subsection (d), with the official specified in subsection (e), and within the time provided in subsection (f). Upon such filing, the secure leave period so designated shall be deemed allowed without further action of the court, and the attorney shall not be required to appear at any argument or other in-court proceeding in the appellate division during that secure leave period.

(d) Content of Designation. The designation shall contain the following information: (1) the attorney's name, address, telephone number, State Bar number, and e-mail address; (2) the date of the Monday on which the secure leave period is to begin and of the Friday on which it is to end; (3) the dates of all other secure leave periods during the current calendar year that have previously been designated by the attorney pursuant to this rule and to Rule 26 of the General Rules of Practice for the Superior and District Courts; (4) a statement that the secure leave period is not being designated for the purpose of delaying, hindering, or interfering with the timely disposition of any matter in any pending action or proceeding; (5) a statement that no argument or other in-court proceeding has been scheduled during the designated secure leave period in any matter pending in the appellate division in which the attorney has entered an appearance; and (6) a listing of all cases, by caption and docket number, pending before the appellate court in which the designation is being filed. The designation shall apply only to those cases pending in that appellate court on the date of its filing. A separate designation shall be filed as to any cases on appeal subsequently filed and docketed.

(e) Where to File Designation. The designation shall be filed as follows: (1) if the attorney has entered an appearance in the Supreme Court, in the office of the clerk of the Supreme Court, even if the designation was filed initially in the Court of Appeals; (2) if the attorney has entered an appearance in the Court of Appeals, in the office of the clerk of the Court of Appeals.

(f) When to File Designation. The designation shall be filed: (1) no later than ninety days before the beginning of the secure leave period, and (2) before any argument or other in-court proceeding has been scheduled for a time during the designated secure leave period.

RULE 34: Frivolous Appeals; Sanctions.

In *Steingress v. Steingress*, 350 N.C. 64, 511 S.E.2d 298 (1999), our Supreme Court noted that the sanctions listed under this rule include dismissal of the appeal and monetary damages, "including, but not limited to, single or double costs, damages occasioned by delay, and reasonable expenses, including reasonable attorney fees, incurred because of the frivolous appeal or proceeding;" and any other sanction deemed just and proper.

If a court of the appellate division deems a sanction appropriate under this rule, the court shall order the person subject to sanction to show cause in writing or in oral argument or both why a sanction should not be imposed. Rule 34(d) does not require an appellate court to hold a special hearing to show cause why a sanction should not be imposed. Rather, under Rule 34(d) an appellant can be required to show cause in writing as enumerated in the rule, or the appellate court can simply demonstrate on the record that during oral arguments, it asked the appellant to show cause why it should not be sanctioned. This inquiry can consist wholly of this one question and need not consume more than a brief part of the oral argument.

Under Rule 34, the appellate courts can sanction a party for a frivolous appeal in certain instances as defined in Rule 34(a). The sanctions can be dismissal of the appeal, monetary damages, or any other just sanction. The appellate court can remand the case back to the trial court to determine appropriate sanctions.

(a) A court of the appellate division may, on its own initiative or motion of a party, impose a sanction against a party or attorney or both when the court determines that an appeal or any proceeding in an appeal was frivolous because of one or more of the following:

(1) the appeal was not well grounded in fact and was not warranted by existing law or a good faith argument for the extension, modification, or reversal of existing law;
(2) the appeal was taken or continued for an improper purpose, such as to harass or to cause unnecessary delay or needless increase in the cost of litigation;
(3) a petition, motion, brief, record, or other paper filed in the appeal was grossly lacking in the requirements of propriety, grossly violated appellate court rules, or grossly disregarded the requirements of a fair presentation of the issues to the appellate court.

(b) A court of the appellate division may impose one or more of the following sanctions:

(1) dismissal of the appeal;

(2) monetary damages including, but not limited to,

a. single or double costs,

b. damages occasioned by delay,

c. reasonable expenses, including reasonable attorney fees, incurred because of the frivolous appeal or proceeding;

(3) any other sanction deemed just and proper.

(c) A court of the appellate division may remand the case to the trial division for a hearing to determine one or more of the sanctions under subdivisions (b)(2) or (b)(3) of this rule.

(d) If a court of the appellate division remands the case to the trial division for a hearing to determine a sanction under subsection (c) of this rule, the person subject to sanction shall be entitled to be heard on that determination in the trial division.

RULE 35: Costs.

This rule is self-explanatory. The appellate clerk will send an invoice for copies made.

(a) To Whom Allowed. Except as otherwise provided by law, if an appeal is dismissed, costs shall be taxed against the appellant unless otherwise agreed by the parties or ordered by the court; if a judgment is affirmed, costs shall be taxed against the appellant unless otherwise ordered by the court; if a judgment is reversed, costs shall be taxed against the appellee unless otherwise ordered; if a judgment is affirmed in part, reversed in part, or modified in any way, costs shall be allowed as directed by the court.

(b) Direction as to Costs in Mandate. The clerk shall include in the mandate of the court an itemized statement of costs taxed in the appellate court and a designation of the party against whom such costs are taxed.

(c) Costs of Appeal Taxable in Trial Tribunals. Any costs of an appeal that are assessable in the trial tribunal shall, upon receipt of the mandate, be taxed as directed therein and may be collected by execution of the trial tribunal.

(d) Execution to Collect Costs in Appellate Courts. Costs taxed in the courts of the appellate division may be made the subject of execution issuing from the court where taxed. Such execution may be directed by the clerk of the court to the proper officers of any county of the state; may be issued at any time after the mandate of the court has been issued; and may be made returnable on any day named. Any officer to whom such execution is directed is subject to the penalties prescribed by law for failure to make due and proper return.

RULE 36: Trial Judges Authorized to Enter Orders Under These Rules.

Under Rule 36, if a trial judge is required to enter a further order, the judges who have authority to do so include the judge who entered the judgment/order appealed from or any regular, special or chief district judge. If that judge is unavailable pursuant to Rule 36(b), the Chief Justice will designate another judge after a party makes a motion.

(a) When Particular Judge Not Specified by Rule. When by these rules a trial court or a judge thereof is permitted or required to enter an order or to take some other judicial action with respect to a pending appeal and the rule does not specify the particular judge with authority to do so, the following judges of the respective courts have such authority with respect to causes docketed in their respective divisions:

(1) Superior Court. The judge who entered the judgment, order, or other determination from which appeal was taken, and any regular or special superior judge resident in the district or assigned to hold court in the district wherein the cause is docketed;

(2) District Court. The judge who entered the judgment, order, or other determination from which appeal was taken; the chief district court judge of the district wherein the cause is docketed; and any judge designated by such chief district court judge to enter interlocutory orders under N.C.G.S. § 7A-192.

(b) Upon Death, Incapacity, or Absence of Particular Judge Authorized. When by these rules the authority to enter an order or to take other judicial action is limited to a particular judge and that judge is unavailable by reason of death, mental or physical incapacity, or absence from the state, the Chief Justice will, upon motion of any party, designate another judge to act in the matter. Such designation will be by order entered ex parte, copies of which will be mailed forthwith by the clerk of the Supreme Court to the judge designated and to all parties.

RULE 37 (above).

RULE 38: Substitution of Parties.

Rule 38 states that an action will not abate even if one of the parties dies. The appeal will continue with a personal representative. Parties also have the ability to substitute parties for reasons other than death. Under Rule 38(c), the action will not abate if it involves the death or separation of a public officer. In *Smith v. State*, 349 N.C. 332, 507 S.E.2d 28 (1998), a substitution was permissible because Janice Faulkner to replaced former defendant Betsy Y. Justus as Secretary of Revenue in 1993. In *In re Higgins*, 160 N.C. App. 704, 587 S.E.2d 77 (2003), however, a cause of action to declare a person incompetent did not survive his death because the result that the petition sought to accomplish was no longer necessary since a guardian was no longer needed, and granting the relief sought would be nugatory after the death.

(a) Death of a Party. No action abates by reason of the death of a party while an appeal may be taken or is pending, if the cause of action survives. If a party acting in an individual capacity dies after appeal is taken from any tribunal, the personal representative of the deceased party in a personal action, or the successor in interest of the deceased party in a real action may be substituted as a party on motion filed by the representative or the successor in interest or by any other party with the clerk of the court in which the action is then docketed. A motion to substitute made by a party shall be served upon the personal representative or successor in interest in addition to all other parties. If such a deceased party in a personal action has no personal representative, any party may in writing notify the court of the death, and the court in which the action is then docketed shall direct the proceedings to be had in order to substitute a personal representative.

If a party against whom an appeal may be taken dies after entry of a judgment or order but before appeal is taken, any party entitled to appeal therefrom may proceed as appellant as if death had not occurred; and after appeal is taken, substitution may then be effected in accordance with this subdivision. If a party entitled to appeal dies before filing a notice of appeal, appeal may be taken by the personal representative, or, if there is no personal representative, by the attorney of record within the time and in the manner prescribed in these rules; and after appeal is taken, substitution may then be effected in accordance with this rule.

(b) Substitution for Other Causes. If substitution of a party to an appeal is necessary for any reason other than death, substitution shall be effected in accordance with the procedure prescribed in subsection (a).

(c) Public Officers; Death or Separation From Office. When a person is a party to an appeal in an official or representative capacity and during its pendency dies, resigns, or otherwise ceases to hold office, the action does not abate and the person's successor is automatically substituted as a party. Prior to the qualification of a successor, the attorney of record for the former party may take any action required by these rules. An order of substitution may be made, but neither failure to enter such an order nor any misnomer in the name of a substituted party shall affect the substitution unless it be shown that the same affected the substantial rights of a party.

RULE 39: Duties of Clerks; When Offices Open.

Rule 39(a) provides that the clerk's offices in the appellate courts will be open during business hours on weekdays, except for holidays. The clerks are sworn under oath. Under Rule 39(b), the clerk's office will maintain and index all records in paper and/or electronic form.

(a) General Provisions. The clerks of the courts of the appellate division shall take the oaths and give the bonds required by law. The courts shall be deemed always open for the purpose of filing any proper paper and of making motions and issuing orders. The offices of the clerks with the clerks or deputies in attendance shall be open during business hours on all days except Saturdays, Sundays, and legal holidays, but the respective courts may provide by order that the offices of their clerks shall be open for specified hours on Saturdays or on particular legal holidays or shall be closed on particular business days.

(b) Records to Be Kept. The clerk of each of the courts of the appellate division shall keep and maintain the records of that court, on paper, microfilm, or electronic media, or any combination thereof. The records kept by the clerk shall include indexed listings of all cases docketed in that court, whether by appeal, petition, or motion, and a notation of the dispositions attendant thereto; a listing of final judgments on appeals before the court, indexed by title, docket number, and parties, containing a brief memorandum of the judgment of the court and the party against whom costs were adjudicated; and records of the proceedings and ceremonies of the court.

RULE 40: Consolidation Of Actions On Appeal.

Under Rule 40, one of the parties can move to consolidate two or more actions on appeal. The actions should involve common issues of law and fact.

Two or more actions that involve common issues of law may be consolidated for hearing upon motion of a party to any of the actions made to the appellate court wherein all are docketed, or upon the initiative of that court. Actions so consolidated will be calendared and heard as a single case. Upon consolidation, the parties may set the course of argument, within the times permitted by Rule 30(b), by written agreement filed with the court prior to oral argument. This agreement shall control unless modified by the court.

RULE 41: Appeal Information Statement.

Under Rule 41, the appellant must fill out an Appeal Information Statement. The statement is mailed to the appellant from the clerk's office. The appellant must complete and return the statement prior to the brief due date. Juvenile names may not be included in the statement.

(a) The Court of Appeals has adopted an Appeal Information Statement (Statement) which will be revised from time to time. The purpose of the Statement is to provide the Court the substance of an appeal and the information needed by the Court for effective case management.

(b) Each appellant shall complete, file, and serve the Statement as set out in this rule.

(1) The clerk of the Court of Appeals shall furnish a Statement form to all parties to the appeal when the record on appeal is docketed in the Court of Appeals.

(2) Each appellant shall complete and file the Statement with the clerk of the Court of Appeals at or before the time his or her appellant's brief is due and shall serve a copy of the statement upon all other parties to the appeal pursuant to Rule 26. The Statement may be filed by mail addressed to the clerk and, if first class mail is utilized, is deemed filed on the date of mailing as evidenced by the proof of service. Parties shall protect the identity of juveniles covered by Rules 3(b)(1), 3.1(b), or 4(e) pursuant to said rules.

(3) If any party to the appeal concludes that the Statement is in any way inaccurate or incomplete, that party may file with the Court of Appeals a written statement setting out additions or corrections within seven days of the service of the Statement and shall serve a copy of the written statement upon all other parties to the appeal pursuant to Rule 26. The written statement may be filed by mail addressed to the clerk and, if first class mail is utilized, is deemed filed on the date of mailing as evidenced by the proof of service.

RULE 42: [RESERVED]

APPENDICES

A.   Certificates of Service

B.   Notices

Of Appeal at the Trial Court (General)
Of Appeal (Juvenile)
Of Appearance

C.   Motions

To Dismiss
At Trial Court Level
At Appellate Court Level
To Extend Deadline
To Consolidate
To Deem Document Timely Filed
To File an Amicus Brief
Memorandum of Additional Authority
Motion Response

D.   Petitions

For Discretionary Review
For Rehearing
Petition Response

E.   Briefs

G.   Tips for Oral Arguments

F.   Appeal Information Statement

APPENDIX A: CERTIFICATES OF SERVICE

CERTIFICATE OF SERVICE

The undersigned hereby certifies that one copy of the foregoing NAME OF DOCUMENT was served by enclosing the same in an envelope, with postage fully prepaid and by depositing said envelope in a United States Post Office mailbox, addressed to:

Attorney Name
Address

Attorney Name
Address

Attorney Name
Address

Attorney Name
Address

This the _____ day of Month 2007.

_____
Name
Bar Number
Address
Telephone Number
Facsimile Number
Email Address
Attorney for ENTER PARTY'S NAME

***Include a Certificate of Service after every document filed at the trial court or appellate court.

APPENDIX B: NOTICES

I. NOTICE OF APPEAL (GENERAL)

STATE OF NORTH CAROLINA   IN THE GENERAL COURT OF JUSTICE
COUNTY OF _____   DISTRICT/SUPERIOR COURT DIVISION

```
Plaintiff                    )
                             )      NOTICE OF APPEAL
v.                           )
                             )
Defendant                    )
```

NOW COMES PARTY NAME, by and through her attorney, YOUR NAME, and gives the court notice that PARTY NAME appeals the SPECIFIC ORDER signed on _____ and entered on _____ by the Honorable JUDGE NAME at the DATE session of the Superior/District Court of _____ County.

_____
Name
Bar Number
Address
Telephone Number
Facsimile Number
Email Address
Attorney for ENTER PARTY'S NAME

II.   NOTICE OF APPEAL (JUVENILE)

STATE OF NORTH CAROLINA   IN THE GENERAL COURT OF JUSTICE
COUNTY OF _____   DISTRICT/SUPERIOR COURT DIVISION

In the Matter of   )
    A.B.C.,   )   NOTICE OF APPEAL
)
)
    Minor child.   )

        NOW COMES PARTY NAME, by and through her attorney, YOUR
NAME, and gives the court notice that PARTY NAME appeals the
SPECIFIC ORDER signed on _____ and entered on _____ by the
Honorable JUDGE NAME at the DATE session of the Superior/District
Court of _____ County.

        This the _____ of MONTH 2008.

        _____
        Appellant Party's Signature

        _____
        Name
        Bar Number
        Address
        Telephone Number
        Facsimile Number
        Email Address
        Attorney for ENTER PARTY'S NAME

III. NOTICE OF APPEARANCE

No. COA_____   JUDICIAL DISTRICT _____

NORTH CAROLINA COURT OF APPEALS

* *

Plaintiff	)	
	)	From _____ County
v.	)	County File Number
	)	
Defendant.	)	

* *
NOTICE OF APPEARANCE OF APPELLATE COUNSEL

* *

PLEASE TAKE NOTE that the undersigned attorney is licensed to practice law in the State of North Carolina and that she desires to make an appearance in this case as appellate counsel for the Plaintiff/Defendant.

This the _____ of MONTH 2008.

_____
Name
Bar Number
Address
Telephone Number
Facsimile Number
Email Address
Attorney for ENTER PARTY'S NAME

APPENDIX C: MOTION WRITING

Motions in the appellate courts are governed by N.C. Appellate Rule 37. This is the appropriate rule to cite in seeking an extension of time. It is also the rule to use if you believe that an appeal is subject to dismissal. Motions may be filed at any time up until the date of the case's hearing. The motion must be written. *Hoyle v. Bagby*, 253 N.C. 778, 780, 117 S.E.2d 760, 761 (1961). Motions may not be in a brief, but instead must be contained in a separate filed document. *Horton v. New South Ins. Co.*, 122 N.C. App. 265, 268, 468 S.E.2d 856, 858, *disc. rev. and cert. denied*, 343 N.C. 511, 472 S.E.2d 8 (1996).

Remember that in your caption, you should be specific about the motion and not just title it "Motion to Dismiss." The caption of your motion to an appellate court should look like this:

NO. COA07-000   5ᵗʰ JUDICIAL DISTRICT

            NORTH CAROLINA COURT OF APPEALS

* *

IN RE A.B.C.,   )   From Wake County
)   07 J 123
        Minor Child.   )

* *
    APPELLEE GUARDIAN AD LITEM'S MOTION TO DISMISS
        APPELLANT'S APPEAL AS INTERLOCUTORY
    *

Just underneath the caption is where you should cite the reason for your motion and list to which rule it is pursuant. For example:

NOW COMES the Guardian ad Litem ("GAL"), pursuant to N.C.G.S. § 7B-1001 and Rule 37 of the North Carolina Rules of Appellate Procedure, and respectfully moves this Court to dismiss Appellant's appeal from the trial court's 21 April 2006 permanency planning order.

After this introduction, it is customary to explain the reasons for the motion in detail in enumerated paragraphs. For example:

1.   Section 7B-1001 provides for a right to appeal from "any final order of the court in a juvenile matter." N.C. Gen. Stat. § 7B-1001 (2005). A "final order" is defined as any order: (1) finding absence of jurisdiction; (2) which determines the action and prevents a judgment from which appeal might be taken; (3) of disposition after an adjudication that a juvenile is abused, neglected, or dependent; or (4) modifying custodial rights. *Id.*

2.   This Court has held that not every juvenile permanency planning order is subject to immediate appeal. *See e.g., In re B.N.H.,* 170 N.C. App. 157, 611 S.E.2d 888 (2005).

3.   The April 21, 2006 permanency planning order in this case does not change custody of the juvenile, nor does it modify Appellant's custodial rights. The order is, therefore, interlocutory in nature and not subject to appeal under N.C.G.S. § 7B-1001.

After the reasons for the motion have been adequately explained, you should end the motion with language indicating that you are respectfully asking the Court to rule in your favor. Remember to be specific with the remedy that you are seeking For example:

For these reasons, the Guardian ad Litem respectfully asks this Court to dismiss Respondent's appeal pursuant to N.C. Gen. Stat. § 7B-1001 of the North Carolina Juvenile Code because the order from which Respondent appeals is interlocutory.

Respectfully submitted this ___ day of Month 2007.

By:
Your Name
Bar Number
Address
Telephone Number
Guardian ad Litem Attorney for Child

You must serve a copy of your motion on every party and include a certificate or service page. Motions may be filed electronically at the appellate courts. N.C.R. App. P. 26 (a). A motion is deemed filed on the date of mailing as evidenced by the proof of service or, if filed by electronic means, at the time it is received electronically. Id. Motions may be filed by facsimile machines, if an oral request for permission to do so has first been tendered to and approved by the clerk of the appropriate appellate court. *Id.*

Service of motions can be accomplished by hand delivery, by mail, or by electronic mail. Service can be accomplished by electronic mail only if the motion was filed electronically. N.C.R. App. P. 26 (c). Service by hand delivery can be made to the attorney of record or the party or by leaving a copy of the motion at the attorney's office with a partner or employee. Id. Service by mail is deemed complete when the motion, enclosed in a postpaid, properly addressed wrapper is deposited in a Post Office or official depository under the exclusive care and custody of the United States Post Office. Id. Service should be at or before the time of filing. N.C.R. App. P. 26(b). A certificate of service indicating the date and manner of service and the person served must be attached to the copy of the motion filed in the appellate court. N.C.R. App. P. 26(d). Absent such a certificate, the appellate court is likely to dismiss the motion. If a motion is supported by affidavits, briefs, or other papers, these shall be served and filed with the motion. N.C.R. App. P. 37(a).

When you get a moment, spend time perusing the Appellate Rules so that you are familiar with them. For every violation you find in your opponent's brief, include it within a motion to dismiss. Frequent circumstances for motions to dismiss include:

1. Parent failing to sign the notice of appeal for juvenile appeals.
2. Opponent's brief filed untimely.
3. Overly argumentative statement of facts.
4. No notice of appeal filed.
5. Appeal is interlocutory.
6. No legal authority cited within the argument.

Other motions directed to the appellate courts include motions for extension of time, motion to treat brief as timely filed, and motion to amend the record on appeal. The captions and body of the motions should look the same as motions to dismiss. Remember to use case law, appellate rules and statutes where applicable.

Responses. A non moving party has 10 days after a motion is served upon him or until the appeal is called for oral argument, whichever period is shorter, to file and serve copies of a response in opposition to the motion. N.C.R. App. P. 37(a). If the motion was served by mail, three additional days are added to the response time pursuant to N.C. R. App. P. 27(b). A response to a motion is considered filed pursuant to N.C. R. App. P. 26(a)(1) when it is received in the clerk's office. The appellate court may shorten or extend the time for responding to a motion either upon request by a party or on its own motion. N.C. R. App. P. 37(a).

The appellate courts routinely rule upon motions for extensions of time ex parte, see N.C. R. App. P. 27(d), and routinely hold motions to dismiss appeal for the requisite response period. Other motions may be ruled upon immediately or held for a response at the discretion of the appellate courts depending upon the specifics of the motions.

The appellate court can also act upon a motion at any time even if not all the parties were given notice and even without waiting for responses. N.C. R. App. P. 37(b). Except in extraordinary circumstances, however, the court is unlikely to allow a motion without affording the adverse parties an opportunity to respond. *See* N.C. R. App. P. 37(b) Drafting Committee Note. If a party did not receive notice of a motion or the appellate court ruled upon a motion without awaiting a response, that part may file a motion for reconsideration, vacation, or modification if adversely affected by the ruling. Id.

Any response to a motion filed in the appellate courts cannot include the name of a juvenile, in compliance with Rule 3(b). N.C. R. App. P. 37(c).

Ruling. The appellate courts endeavor to rule upon motions in a prompt fashion. The amount of time it takes to obtain a ruling depends on whether the motion is held for a response and on the complexity of the motion. Motions for the extension of time (except those held for responses) are often ruled upon by the next business day after receipt by the appellate court, but they sometimes take longer. Motions that are held for a response typically are ruled upon within a few days after all responses have been received or after the response time has expired.

At the Court of Appeals, motions filed after a case has been calendared may not be ruled upon as promptly as those filed before calendaring. Depending on the type of motion filed, motions filed after a case has been calendared may not be ruled upon until the panel assigned to the case has filed an opinion.

Motions to dismiss an appeal filed in the Court of Appeals take longer for a ruling because they are held for a response and because the rulings are made with much deliberation. If the Court chooses to make a final determination on a motion to dismiss appeal rather than entering an interim order referring to the motion to the panel assigned after the case is calendared, it will ordinarily try to do so prior to any then existing deadlines for the filing of briefs by the parties.

When it is apparent that the Court will not be able to rule upon a motion to dismiss appeal prior to the deadline for the filing of a brief (because of the required) response time or some other reason), the party who is to file that brief should file a motion for extension of time in order to avoid the potential waste of time and money in drafting and filing the brief. The party could ask for an extension of a certain length or to be allowed to file a certain amount of days after the Court has ruled on the motion to dismiss. Even if an extension is granted until a certain number of days after a ruling is made on the motion to dismiss, the party seeking the extension should be aware that an order of the Court referring the motion to the panel assigned to the case is a "ruling" which begins the time running for the filing of the brief.

Meanings of Rulings.

Allowed: if the Appellate Court simply "allows" the motion, the requests in the motion are considered to have been granted in full. However, appellate court rulings commonly include additional language explaining or limiting the ruling. For example, the motion for extension of time may be "allowed," but additional language in the order may indicate that only a portion of the time requested has been granted

Denied: the appellate court has ruled upon the motion on its merits. Occasionally, a motion will be "denied without prejudice to refile" upon the fulfillment of certain conditions. The appellate courts do not ordinarily explain in an order why a motion was denied.

Dismissed: A dismissal is not a ruling on the merits of a motion. Instead, a dismissal indicates that the appellate court will not consider the motion for one of a number of reasons. Some of those reasons—the appellate court's lack of jurisdiction is one example—may not be correctable. Other reasons—the motion is premature or some other prerequisite for filing has not been met—are probably correctable. The appellate court's order may not explain the reason for the dismissal but occasionally will specify that the motion has been "dismissed without prejudice" upon the fulfillment of certain conditions

Referred: At the Court of Appeals, some motions are "referred to the panel to which the case is assigned." This interim ruling means the ultimate disposition of the motion is deferred until all briefs have been filed and the case has been calendared. The panel of judges assigned to hear the appeal will then rule upon the motion while it has the entire case under consideration and may not do so until the opinion is filed. There is no reason to contact the Clerk's Office inquiring as to a ruling on the motion if the case has not yet been assigned to a panel for hearing.

This interim hearing is made most often with regard to motions to dismiss appeal. However, the ruling is not automatic when a motion to dismiss has been made. The Court of Appeals strives to dispose of motions to dismiss appeal at the earliest time in order to spare the parties the expense and time of filing briefs if this is unnecessary. The interim deferral is made only when the Court of Appeals believes a more thorough consideration of the entire case is needed before entering a ruling on a motion to dismiss. Since an appellee may file a motion to dismiss an appeal prior to the filing of its brief (or even prior to the filing of the appellant's brief), the practical effect of the interim ruling is that all briefs, including appellee's brief, must be filed before a final ruling is made.

Please see the samples on the following pages.

I.   **MOTION TO DISMISS (Trial Level)**

```
STATE OF NORTH CAROLINA          IN THE GENERAL COURT OF JUSTICE
COUNTY OF ORANGE                 DISTRICT COURT DIVISION


IN THE MATTER OF:

                                   MOTION TO DISMISS APPEAL

A.A.A.,
     Minor child.
```

NOW COMES Counsel for the juvenile as appellee, on behalf of the juvenile in this matter, pursuant to Rules 3A and 37 of the North Carolina Appellate Procedure and moves the Court for a dismissal of the appeal of Respondent Mother for failure to timely sign the Notice of Appeal. In support of this Motion, Counsel shows the following:

1. The trial court filed an order terminating Appellant's parental rights to the above-named juvenile on 14 February 2008.

2. Appellant did not file a notice of appeal until 20 March 2008.

3. Pursuant to the expedited Rules of Appellate Procedure in juvenile cases, Appellant had until 14 March 2008, or 30 days, to timely file a notice of appeal.

4. It is well-established that "failure to give timely notice of appeal … is jurisdictional, and an untimely attempt to appeal must be dismissed." *In re A.L.*, 166 N.C. App. 276, 277, 601 S.E.2d 538, 538 (2004) (citations omitted).

5. The Notice of Appeal does not comply with the requirements of Rule 3A and this case is devoid of a properly executed notice of appeal that was timely filed.

WHEREFORE, Counsel for the Guardian ad Litem respectfully requests that this Court dismiss the appeal and grant other relief this Court deems just and proper.

This the _____ day of Month 2007.

                          _____
                          Your Name
                          Your Bar Number
                          Your Address
                          Your Telephone Number
                          Your Facsimile Number
                          Your Email Address
                          Attorney for ENTER PARTY'S NAME

II. MOTION TO DISMISS (Appellate Level)

No. COA_____   JUDICIAL DISTRICT THREE B

NORTH CAROLINA COURT OF APPEALS

****

Plaintiff)) v.)) Defendant)	From County File 06 CVS 90

****
MOTION TO DISMISS APPEAL
****

Comes Now, the Appellant Attorney, pursuant to the North Carolina Rules of Appellate Procedure, Rules 3A, 25, 26, 27, and 37 and moves this Honorable Court to dismiss the appeal in the above-captioned matter for failures to comply with the North Carolina Rules of Appellate Procedure. In support of this motion, Appellees respectfully submit the following:

1.   The trial court filed an order on 4 April 2007.

2.   After the transcript was delivered, Appellant mailed all parties the proposed record on appeal on 31 May 2007. (See Exhibit A).

3.   Pursuant to the Rules of Appellate Procedure, Appellant had until 1 July 2007 to file the record on appeal to this Court.

5.   Nonetheless, Appellant did not mail the record on appeal to this Court until 5 July 2007. It was not received by this Court

or the parties until 9 July 2007. Consequently, the record on appeal was 21 days late.

6. After verifying with the Clerk of the Court of Appeals on the morning of 9 July 2007 that no appellate record had been filed, undersigned counsel filed a Motion to Dismiss Appeal with the District Court and mailed copies to all counsel on July 9th, with a hearing notice for 23 August 2007. Coincidentally, the appellant's late filing with the Court of Appeals arrived by mail this same day. The trial court hearing of the motion to dismiss was later continued to 7 September 2007. However, it is our position that Appellant's Motion to Deem the Record Timely Filed should be denied.

7. Juvenile appeals "shall adhere strictly to the expedited procedures set forth [in Rule 3A]." N.C. R. App. P. 3A(b). Failure to take any action within the prescribed timelines in the Rules of Appellate Procedure subjects the appeal to dismissal. N.C. R. App. P. 25(a). The Rules of Appellate Procedure are "mandatory and failure to follow these rules will subject an appeal to dismissal." *In re Riddle*, ___ N.C. App. ___ 637 S.E.2d 239 (2006) (quoting *Viar v. N.C. Dept. of Transp.*, 359 N.C. 353, 626 S.E. 2d 270 (2006) (appeal dismissed for failure to attach a certificate of service to the notice of appeal)).

8. The mandatory nature of the Rules of Appellate Procedure applies equally to child protection matters. *See In re: C.T. and B.T.*, ___ N.C. App. ___, 641 S.E.2d 414 (2007) (appeal from an abuse and neglect order dismissed on same grounds).

9. In the instant matter, the District Court entered a final

order terminating parental rights on 4 April 2007. The respondent-father thereafter filed a notice of appeal. (See Exhibit B).

10. On 18 May 2007, Tamara W. Norton, Transcriber, timely delivered and/or mailed the transcript of the TPR hearing to all parties. (See Exhibit A). On 31 May 2007 (the last possible day), Appellant mailed all counsel the proposed record on appeal. Pursuant to Rule 3A, any objections or amendments were due by 11 June 2007. DSS and Guardian ad Litem timely replied. D.S.S. sent Appellant and all other parties a response requesting minor amendments (corrections of typographical errors only) on 7 June 2007. (See Exhibit C).

11. The outside date within which appellant was required to file either the settled or a proposed record was within five business days of the last day upon which the record could have been settled by agreement. That settlement date was 11 June 2007. Thus, appellant's filing of the record was due by 18 June 2007.

12. Appellant's sole basis for requesting relief is due to counsel's miscalculation of the deadline. Whereas the undersigned counsel timely filed a response to the proposed record requesting only the correction of typographical errors, no good cause exists as to why Appellant could not have timely filed the appeal notwithstanding counsel's miscalculation.

13. The appellant cites Rule 2 as the basis for excusing the failure to meet the strict timelines of Rule 3A. However, appellant cites no hardship or tragedy that prevented him from timely filing the record on appeal.

14. Moreover, suspending the rules to permit this inexcusable delay results in manifest injustice to the subject child, whose permanency has already been delayed by Appellant's actions.

15. Appellant failed to timely file a record on appeal, and that failure should result in dismissal of the appeal.

16. In addition, the notice of appeal in the record does not comply with Rule 3A because it does not carry the signature of the father, and its accompanying certificate of service at does not include service upon counsel for the mother. (See Exhibit D and R. p. 59, 96).

17. Pursuant to Rule 3A, "if the appellant is represented by counsel, both the trial counsel and appellant must sign the notice of appeal…." N.C. R. App. P. 3A. As noted above, parties must strictly adhere to the requirements of Rule 3A and any failure – including a missing certificate of service – subjects the appeal to dismissal.

18. Appellant has failed to meet the mandatory provisions of the North Carolina Rules of Appellate Procedure, and the appeal should be dismissed.

WHEREFORE, Appellees Carteret County D.S.S. and Guardian ad Litem pray that this Court will immediately deny Appellant's Motion to Deem Record Timely Filed and dismiss this appeal.

Respectfully submitted this the 13th day of July 2007.

19. Nonetheless, Appellant did not mail the record on appeal to this Court until 5 July 2007. It was not received by this Court or the parties until 9 July 2007.

20. Failure to take any action within the prescribed timelines in the Rules of Appellate Procedure subjects the appeal to dismissal. N. C. R. App. P. 25(a). The Rules of Appellate Procedure are "mandatory and failure to follow these rules will subject an appeal to dismissal." *In re Riddle*, ___ N.C. App. ___ 637 S.E.2d 239 (2006) (quoting *Viar v. N.C. Dept. of Transp.*, 359 N.C. 353, 626 S.E. 2d 270 (2006) (appeal dismissed for failure to attach a certificate of service to the notice of appeal)).

21. Appellant has failed to meet the mandatory provisions of the North Carolina Rules of Appellate Procedure, and the appeal should be dismissed.

WHEREFORE, Appellee prays that this Court will immediately deny Appellant's Motion to Deem Record Timely Filed and dismiss this appeal.

Respectfully submitted this the ____ day of ___ 2007.

_____

Name
Bar Number
Address
Telephone Number
Facsimile Number
Email Address
Attorney for PARTY'S NAME

III. MOTION TO EXTEND DEADLINE

No. COA08-1234   JUDICIAL DISTRICT 9

NORTH CAROLINA COURT OF APPEALS

* *

Plaintiff   )
)   <u>From County</u>
v.   )   File Number
)
Defendants.   )

* *
MOTION FOR EXTENSION OF TIME
TO RESPOND TO APPELLANT'S BRIEF
* *

NOW COMES Appellee, by and through appellate counsel, pursuant to Rule 14(a)(1) of the North Carolina Rules of Appellate Procedure, and respectfully move this Court for an extension of time to respond to Appellant's brief. In support of this motion, Appellees show the following:

1.   On February 28, 2005, Appellants filed a notice of appeal in the above-captioned matter.

2.   On January 3, 2006, Appellant served his appellate brief in this matter and, pursuant to Rule 13 of the North Carolina Rules of Appellate Procedure, Appellees' response to Appellant's brief is due on February 6, 2006. The second Appellant's brief is due on 8 February 2006

3.   Appellee anticipate that, in addressing both Appellants' assignments of error in one, single brief, additional time is

needed. Filing one, single brief in response to Appellants' briefs will further the interests of judicial economy and will enable Appellee to more effectively address the issues raised on appeal.

Appellees have not previously requested any extensions of time in this matter.

For these reasons, Appellees respectfully ask this Court to grant their motion for an extension of time to respond to Appellant brief for 30 days from the date of service. Appellees also ask this Court to grant them leave to file a single brief in response to both Appellants' briefs in excess of the 8,750 word limit, but in no event more than 15,500 words.

Respectfully submitted this _____ day of January, 2006.

IV.   MOTION TO CONSOLIDATE

No. COA07-9   JUDICIAL DISTRICT 1

NORTH CAROLINA COURT OF APPEALS

****

Plaintiff	)	
v.	)	From County
Defendant.	)	File Number

****

MOTION TO CONSOLIDATE APPEALS

****

NOW COMES the Appellate Counsel respectfully moves this Court to consolidate the appeals in this matter. In support of this motion, GAL respectfully submits the following:

1.   The first order was signed on ____ and filed on _____ .

2.   Respondent(s) appealed from the first order on _____ .

3.   The second order was signed on __ and filed on _____ .

4.   Respondent(s) appealed from the second order on _____ .

5.   Both appeals concern the same parties and subject matter. It would be reasonable and efficient for the Court of Appeals to consider them together on appeal.

For these reasons, Counsel respectfully asks this Court to consolidate these appeals.

Respectfully submitted this the ____ day of ___ 2007.

_____

Name
Bar Number
Address
Telephone Number
Facsimile Number
Email Address
Attorney for PARTY'S NAME

V.   MOTION TO DEEM BRIEF TIMELY FILED

No. COA07-1432   JUDICIAL DISTRICT FIFTEEN-B

NORTH CAROLINA COURT OF APPEALS

IN THE MATTER OF:)
)   From Orange County
X.Y.Z.,   )   06 JA 179
Minor child.   )   06 JA 180

****
MOTION TO DEEM BRIEF TIMELY FILED
****

NOW COMES Counsel for Guardian ad Litem, as appellee, pursuant to Rules 3A and 37 of the North Carolina Appellate Procedure and moves the Court to deem GAL's appellee's brief timely filed for extraordinary circumstances. In support of this Motion, the GAL shows the following:

1.   Respondent Appellant appealed from an adjudication order of the trial court on 17 July 2007. She appealed a disposition order on 23 October 2007. (Exhibit A)

2.   The Orange County Superior Court Clerk promptly notified the AOC court reporting coordinator, who set up the transcription properly, pursuant to Rule 3A of the N.C. Rules of Appellate Procedure.

3.   The State Office contacted the Attorney in this case, who stated that she would complete a joint brief with DSS for this appeal. An approval letter to bill for time working on the brief was sent to the attorney on 6 August 2007. (Exhibit B)

4.   The attorney was timely served with the Record on Appeal, which was filed on 26 November 2007, and Respondent's brief, which was filed 5 December 2007. (Exhibit C) The State attorney did not participate with DSS, which filed its brief on 29 January 2008. At no time prior to 21 February 2008 did the attorney inform the State Office or local office that she was not participating in the appeal. (Exhibit D)

5.   On 21 February 2008, Respondent's Appellate Counsel contacted the State Office about the appeal and questioned whether the undersigned had any knowledge that DSS had asserted that the juvenile was not a party to the appeal.

6.   The undersigned immediately followed up with the Attorney, who stated that she did not advocate for the juveniles in this case by authoring a brief or a joint brief with DSS. The undersigned, who participates in most of the GAL appeals in the state, immediately filed the following motions: (1) a motion to substitute the undersigned for the Attorney as Appellate Counsel for the juveniles; (2) a notice of appearance; (3) a response to Respondent's motion for sanctions and to strike the DSS brief; and (4) a response to the DSS response that the juvenile is not a party to the appeal.

7.   The undersigned is aware that the brief is very late, especially for the expedited appellate rules in juvenile cases. However, the undersigned asks that this Court consider the brief because the juveniles in this case deserve to be represented by competent appellate counsel. The failure of the juveniles' previous representation on appeal constitutes extraordinary circumstances.

WHEREFORE, Counsel for the Guardian ad Litem respectfully requests that this Court allow this brief to be filed and deemed timely and grant other relief this Court deems just and proper.

This the _____ of MONTH 2008.

Name
Bar Number
Address
Telephone Number
Facsimile Number
Email Address
Attorney for ENTER PARTY'S NAME

VI.   MOTION TO FILE AN AMICUS BRIEF

No. 90A200   JUDICIAL DISTRICT 1

                    SUPREME COURT OF NORTH CAROLINA

Plaintiff   )
)
)   From County
v.   )   File Number
)
Defendant.   )

* *
            MOTION FOR LEAVE TO FILE AMICUS CURIAE BRIEF
* *

The Organization, pursuant to Rule 18(i) of the North
Carolina Rules of Appellate Procedure, respectfully requests
the Court for leave to file an amicus curiae brief in the above-
captioned matter. In support of its motion, the Organization
states as follows:

1.   The Organization is the entity charged with the
oversight of the items in controversy.

2.   The above-captioned matter squarely addresses the
issue of whether the trial court retains jurisdiction to hear and
determine the outcome of a case involving these items while an
appeal of an earlier hearing in the cause is pending.

3.   The outcome of this appeal is extremely important to the
Organization because _____

4.   A copy of the proposed Amicus Curiae Brief is attached
hereto.

For these reasons, the Organization respectfully asks this

134

Court grant its motion to file an amicus curiae brief in this case.

Respectfully submitted, This the _____ of MONTH 2008.

_____
Name
Bar Number
Address
Telephone Number
Facsimile Number
Email Address
Attorney for ENTER PARTY'S NAME

VII. MEMORANDUM OF ADDITIONAL AUTHORITY

No. 297A07   TWENTIETH JUDICIAL DISTRICT

NORTH CAROLINA SUPREME COURT

****

IN THE MATTER OF:	)	From Guilford County
A.B. and C.D.,	)	04 JT 1005
Minor Children.	)	04 JT 1127

****
MEMORANDUM OF ADDITIONAL AUTHORITY
****

NOW COMES Cunsel for the Appellant, and pursuant to N.C. Rule of Procedure 28(g), submits this Memorandum of Additional Authority and cites the decision of the of the North Carolina Court of Appeals in *In re DM, BM and AM*, ___ N.C. App. ___, 647 S.E.2d 689 (2007) (unpublished), as reaffirming the principle that since the parent did not raise any objection to the GAL's performance of her duties, the N.C. Court of Appeals was precluded from reviewing the issue.

Although it is unpublished, the *DM, et al.* case is directly on point and relevant to the issues on appeal. It is attached as Exhibit A.

Respectfully submitted, this the _____ of MONTH 2008.

_____
Name
Bar Number
Address
Telephone Number
Facsimile Number
Email Address
Attorney for ENTER PARTY'S NAME

VIII. MOTION RESPONSE

No. COAP08-1234
FIVE

JUDICIAL DISTRICT

NORTH CAROLINA COURT OF APPEALS

* *

Plaintiff	)	
	)	<u>From County</u>
v.	)	07 CVS 456
	)	
Defendant	)	

* *
* *

RESPONSE TO APPELLANT'S MOTION TO EXTEND TIME
TO SERVE PROPOSED RECORD ON APPEAL

* *
* *

Comes Now, Appellate Counsel representing the above-named Plaintiff, pursuant to the North Carolina Rules of Appellate Procedure, Rules 25, 26, 27, and 37 and opposes the Appellant's Motion to Extend Time to Serve Proposed Record on Appeal. In support of this motion, Appellee respectfully submits the following:

1. The trial court filed an order on 21 November 2007.

2. Appellant filed a Notice of Appeal on 20 December 2007.

3. The transcript was delivered on 17 January 2008.

4. Pursuant to the Rules of Appellate Procedure Appellant has until 22 April 2008 to serve the proposed record on appeal to all parties. N.C. R. App. P. 11.

5. Appellant filed a Motion to Extend Time to Serve completed."

6. Appellant's sole basis for requesting relief is due to Appellant's failure to sign the Notice of Appeal as expected. Trial counsel did not mail the notice to Appellant to sign until 21 April 2008. The undersigned will not oppose any Motion to Amend the Record on Appeal to include information regarding the additional Notice of Appeal. However, the Appellant has not shown any hardship or tragedy which will prevent her from timely serving the proposed record on appeal. Moreover, suspending the rules to permit this delay results in manifest injustice to the subject in controversy.

7. Failure to take any action within the prescribed timelines in the Rules of Appellate Procedure subjects the appeal to dismissal. N.C. R. App. P. 25(a).

8. Thus, it is the undersigned's position that the Motion should be denied.

WHEREFORE, Appellee prays that this Court will immediately deny Appellant's Motion to Extend Time to Serve Proposed Record On Appeal.

Respectfully submitted this the __ day of Month 2008.

Name
Bar Number
Address
Telephone Number
Facsimile Number
Email Address
Attorney for ENTER PARTY'S NAME

APPENDIX D: PETITIONS

I. PETITION FOR DISCRETIONARY REVIEW

NO. P07-789

FIFTH DISTRICT

SUPREME COURT OF NORTH CAROLINA

PLAINTIFF	)	From County
	)	No. COA06-555
V.	)	
	)	
DEFENDANT	)	

****

PETITION FOR DISCRETIONARY REVIEW

****

COMES NOW the Petitioner, pursuant to N.C.R. App. P. 15(a), and hereby submits a Petition for Discretionary Review under N.C. Gen. Stat. § 7A-31 and Appellate Rule 15.

PROCEDURAL BACKGROUND

This Petition concerns the _____. Discuss the procedural background of the case.

REASONS WHY CERTIFICATION SHOULD ISSUE

I. THIS CASE INVOLVES LEGAL PRINCIPLES OF MAJOR SIGNIFICANCE TO THE JURISPRUDENCE OF THE STATE.

Discretionary review of a Court of Appeals' decision may be had when in the opinion of the Supreme Court:

(1) The subject matter of the appeal has significant public interest; or

(2) The cause involves legal principles of major significance to the jurisprudence of the State; or

(3) The decision of the Court of

Appeals appears likely to be in conflict with
a decision of the Supreme Court.

N.C. Gen. Stat. § 7A-31(c).

In sum, this matter does not involve legal principles of major significance to the jurisprudence of this State, and the Petition should be denied.

THIS CASE DOES NOT MEET ANY OF THE OTHER CRITERIA FOR PETITIONING FOR DISCRETIONARY REVIEW.

Petitioner has not raised, nor does the case meet, any of the other criteria to support a petition for discretionary review. Under N.C. Gen. Stat. § 7A-31(c), discretionary review also may be permitted when "[t]he subject matter of the appeal has significant public interest" or when "[t]he decision of the Court of Appeals appears likely to be in conflict with a decision of the Supreme Court." The decision in this matter does not meet either criterion.

The decision is not a matter of significant public interest. The decision does not raise any constitutional issues, change public policy, or create new standards of law. Further, the decision is in line with other opinions by both this Court and the Court of Appeals. The application of law to the unique facts of this case only affects those directly involved and not the public as a whole.

As such, the Petition should be denied.

CONCLUSION

Petitioner has established the essential elements of a petition for discretionary review under N.C. Gen. Stat. § 7A-31. Accordingly, the Petition for Discretionary Review should be granted.

Respectfully submitted this the __ day of Month 2008.

_____

Name
Bar Number
Address
Telephone Number
Facsimile Number
Email Address
Attorney for ENTER PARTY'S NAME

II.   PETITION FOR REHEARING

No. COA06-13   TWENTY-SECOND JUDICIAL DISTRICT

NORTH CAROLINA COURT OF APPEALS

****

IN THE MATTER OF:	)	
	)	<u>From County</u>
L.M.N.	)	07 JT 1005
Minor child.	)	

****

PETITION FOR REHEARING

****

NOW COMES the minor child, by and through her Guardian ad Litem Appellate Counsel, and respectfully moves this Court to rehear this appeal pursuant to Rule 31 of the N.C. Rules of Appellate Procedure due to this Court's inadvertent misapprehension of the laws and facts surrounding this appeal. In support of this petition, Guardian ad litem respectfully submits the following:

I.   THE COURT DID NOT HAVE JURISDICTION TO DETERMINE THE QUESTIONS DISCUSSED IN THE OPINION.

This Court filed an opinion in the instant case _____. The opinion did not reach the merits of the case, but addressed procedural issues which were not properly before the Court. It is clearly established that issues on appeal must be limited to issues arising out of the order from which the appeal flows. *Walker v. Fleetwood Homes of North Carolina, Inc.*, 176 N.C. App. 668, 627 S.E.2d 629, *cert. denied*, 360 N.C. 545, 635 S.E.2d 62 (2006). When an order is not appealed, this Court has no jurisdiction to consider issues arising out of the order. *Von Ramm v. Von Ramm*, 99 N.C. App. 153, 156-57, 392 S.E.2d 422, 424-25 (1990).

Moreover, Appellant failed to object or make a motion at trial to preserve the issues. N.C.R. App. P. 10(b)(1). Because the Court's scope of review is limited to proper assignments of error, these questions should have been dismissed by the Court. 638 S.E.2d

626, ___ (2007) (citing N.C.R. App. P. 10(b)(1)).

II. THIS COURT MISAPPREHENDED THE FACTS OF THE INSTANT CASE.

Even if this Court is not persuaded by the previous argument, this petition for rehearing should be granted because the majority misapprehended the facts of this case. *See* N.C. R. App. P. 31. In the opinion, the majority reversed the trial the prior adjudicatory and dispositional hearings, Appellant did not object to the guardian ad litem who was representing the children at the time and never objected to different guardians ad litem representing the children.

In *In re L.L.*, 172 N.C. App. 689, 694, 616 S.E.2d 392, 380-81 (2005), this Court held that because the appellants did not object to a specific judge's calendaring, the issue was not properly preserved for appellate review. The only reason this Court reviewed the merits of *L.L.* was because the issue concerned subject matter jurisdiction, which may be brought as an issue at any time. *Id.* Subject matter jurisdiction is not the case for issues involving the appointment, duration or changing of a guardian ad litem.

Likewise, in *In re J.B.*, 172 N.C. App. 1, 616 S.E.2d 264 (2005), this Court did not reach the question of whether a therapist could testify about a diagnosis because the appellant in that case failed to "object[] during the hearing to either of the witnesses' qualifications, and, on appeal, [did] not point to any testimony by the witnesses admitted over her objection." *Id.* at 19-20, 616 S.E.2d at 275. *See also In re A.E. and J.E.*, 171 N.C. App. 675, 615 S.E.2d 53 (2005) (Court held that appellant's question on expert testimony was not properly before it because appellant failed to object or argue this question at trial); *In re O.W.*, 164 N.C. App. 699, 596 S.E.2d 851 (2004) (holding that the question of consolidating the adjudication and disposition hearings was not properly before the Court because the appellant failed to object at trial). Therefore, pursuant to *D.R.S.*, and N.C.R. App. P. 10(b)(1), the scope of review of the instant case could not have included the above arguments. The majority misapprehended the facts of the instant case. Explain why.

III. THIS COURT MISAPPREHENDED THE APPLICABLE LAW IN THE INSTANT CASE.

A. Prejudice

This Court has held, in *In re R.A.H.*, 171 N.C. App. at 431, 614 S.E.2d at 385, that prejudice is presumed where "a child [is] not represented by a guardian ad litem at a critical stage of the termination proceedings." A guardian ad litem is not required where the petition alleges only dependency. *Id.*

B.   Section 7B-601(a).

The duties delineated in section 7B-601(a) are directed at the Guardian ad Litem Program. *See* N.C. Gen. Stat. § 7B-601(a). In the instant case, the majority misapprehended the meaning of section 7B-601(a) when it concluded that the trial court violated this statute by failing to appoint a GAL to represent either child upon the filing of a petition alleging neglect.

CONCLUSION

For these reasons, the juvenile, by and through his Counsel, believes that this Court has acted under a misapprehension of the law and facts in this case and respectfully asks this Court to grant this petition to rehear this case pursuant to N.C. R. App. P. 31, with oral arguments to better clarify the issues. In addition, Counsel asks that the mandate of this Court be stayed so as to preserve time to appeal to the N.C. Supreme Court should this petition be denied.

Respectfully submitted this the ___ day of Month 2008.

_____

Name
Bar Number
Address
Telephone Number
Facsimile Number
Email Address
Attorney for ENTER PARTY'S NAME

CERTIFICATE

The undersigned hereby certifies that he/she has been a member of the bar of this State for at least five years. The undersigned has no interest in the subject of this action and has not been counsel for any party to this action. The undersigned has carefully examined the appeal and the authorities cited in the decision, and considers the decision in error on points specifically and concisely identified.

This the _____ day of Month 2008.

_____
Name
Bar Number
Address
Telephone Number
Facsimile Number
Email Address
Attorney for ENTER PARTY'S NAME

_____
Attorney for ENTER PARTY'S NAME

CERTIFICATE

The undersigned hereby certifies that he/she has been a member of the bar of this State for at least five years. The undersigned has no interest in the subject of this action and has not been counsel for any party to this action. The undersigned has carefully examined the appeal and the authorities cited in the decision, and considers the decision in error on points specifically and concisely identified.

This the ___ day of Month 2008.

_____
Name
Bar Number
Address
Telephone Number
Facsimile Number
Email Address

Respectfully submitted this the __ day of Month 2008.

_____
Name
Bar Number
Address
Telephone Number
Facsimile Number
Email Address
Attorney for ENTER PARTY'S NAME

III.   RESPONSE TO PETITION

No. COAP08-170   TWENTY-SIXTH JUDICIAL DISTRICT

NORTH CAROLINA COURT OF APPEALS

* *

Plaintiff	)	<u>From County</u>
	)	08 CVS 1111
v.	)	
	)	
Defendant.	)	

RESPONSE TO PETITION FOR WRIT OF CERTIORARI

NOW COMES Counsel pursuant to Rules 21(d) and 37 of the North Carolina Rules of Appellate Procedure and responds to the petition for writ of certiorari. In support of this Motion, Counsel shows the following:

1.   The trial court entered an order on _____. Defendant filed a notice of appeal. However, there was no final order in place from which Defendant could appeal. In *In re Hawkins*, 120 N.C. App. 585, 463 S.E.2d 268 (1995), this Court held that an oral notice of appeal immediately after the termination was not an appeal of a final order. Therefore this Court dismissed the appeal.

2.   Likewise, in the instant case, no findings of fact or conclusions of law were entered by the trial court on the date of the hearing. The trial court's oral termination was not a final order because its "announcement in open court was not yet final as to be suitable for appellate review. The findings of fact and conclusions of law were not set forth in final form[.]" *Id.* at 589, 463 S.E.2d at 271 (citing *In re Hayes*, 106 N.C. App. 652, 418 S.E.2d 304; *Cobb v. Rocky Mount Board of Education*, 102 N.C. App. 681, 403 S.E.2d 538 (1991), *aff'd*, 331 N.C. 280, 415 S.E.2d 554 (1992)).

3.   Because the final order was not entered until 18 January 2008, Respondent Mother could not have appealed before that date. Neither did she appeal after that date, referencing the final order,

within the mandatory time limits.

4.   It is well-established that "failure to give timely notice of appeal … is jurisdictional, and an untimely attempt to appeal must be dismissed." *In re A.L.*, 166 N.C. App. 276, 277, 601 S.E.2d 538, 538 (2004) (citations omitted). Thus, a defective notice of appeal deprives this Court of jurisdiction, which cannot be waived.

5.   Therefore, Plaintiff respectfully asks that Defendant's writ of certiorari be denied.

           _____

           Name
           Bar Number
           Address
           Telephone Number
           Facsimile Number
           Email Address
           Attorney for ENTER PARTY'S NAME

APPENDIX E: BRIEFS

Outlining and Organization

Begin early! One of the worst mistakes an appellate attorney can make is to wait until the appellant's brief has arrived before commencing the appellee brief. This is a scary risk to take. There is no excuse for a late brief. In addition, the appellee will miss out on motion filing prime time. Thus, **do not** wait until you have received the appellant's brief to begin preparing the case. Especially with the new expedited appellate procedure, make sure to look through the file early on. As soon as you get the notice of appeal, scrutinize it for any mistakes. If the appeal has not been perfected within time limitations, file a motion to dismiss at the trial court. Review the record on appeal, assignments of error and transcript, speak with the trial attorney or the district administrator if you have any questions about the facts or procedure.

***Make sure the record on appeal has all of the previous orders included.

Get organized and keep track of your timelines. A good idea is to keep a chart on a separate piece of paper in the front of the file in your office. Calculate all of the timelines so that you know ahead of time when a filing is late. Here is a sample timeline:

Item	Date Received	Due Date
Transcript	1/1/2008	
Proposed Record on Appeal		
Objections and Amendments		
Record on Appeal	4/20/2008	
Appellant Brief	5/20/2008	
Appellee Brief		6/20/2008

By keeping the chart updated, you save yourself time that you would spend calculating and re-calculating timelines.

After familiarizing yourself with the file, recognize what needs to go in the statement of the case and what should be left for the statement of the facts. The statement of the case should include only procedural matters, such as what order was entered on what date. The statement of the facts should be much longer and include what was going on in the lives of the family members during the proceedings. It is all right for some overlap between the two sections. Make sure you report each hearing and each document filed in the statement of the case.

Go ahead and draft the caption, statement of the case and statement of the facts. Remember that the new rules require the use of a juvenile's initials; however it is okay to use a pseudonym.

NORTH CAROLINA COURT OF APPEALS

* *

Plaintiff   From Wake County
    v.   07 CRS 123
Defendant

* *

DEFENDANT APPELLANT's BRIEF

* *

The Pre-Writing Stage

Take time to organize and outline your thoughts. Think about the format of the document you are drafting. Review the N.C. Rules of Appellate Procedure requirements for appellee's briefs. You must include the following:

    i.   Index
   ii.   Table of Authorities
  iii.   Argument(s)
   iv.   Conclusion
    v.   Identification of counsel
   vi.   Proof of service
  vii.   **Note: No questions presented, no statement of the case, statement of the facts, statement of the grounds for appellate review or statement of the standard of review are required <u>unless</u> you disagree with the appellant's statements.

Remember that even if other parties file separate briefs, you should combine any assignments of error which address the same issues. Due to the expedited appeal process for juvenile matters, the law clerks and judges have a reduced amount of time to study the briefs before the opinion needs to be filed. Keep in mind that it is easier for the law clerk and judge to follow the arguments if you put them in the same order as the appellant. Schedule extra time to respond to a poorly written brief; they are frequently the most difficult to which to respond.

Drafting the brief

Remember the Four Cs: Be <u>C</u>lear, Be <u>C</u>oncise, <u>C</u>onvey the point, and <u>C</u>heck your work.

Write <u>clearly.</u> When writing, attorneys tend to lean heavily on legalese, even when it is not necessary. It is important to keep your writing simple for clarity. Remember to use the minimum number of sentences and words possible and to use plain English. A good authority on this point is Bryan A Garner, <u>Legal Writing in Plain English</u> (2001) or Richard C. Wydick, <u>Plain English for Lawyers</u> (5th Ed. 2005). Both of these authors emphasize better wording. For example, Garner lists wordy phrases and how to simplify them:

Bloated Phrase	Normal Expression
An adequate number of	Enough
A number of	Many, several
A sufficient number of	Enough
At the present time	Now
At the point when	When
At this point in time	Now
During such time as	While
During the course of	During
For the reason that	Because
In the event that	If
In the near future	Soon
Is able to	Can
Notwithstanding the fact that	Although
On a daily basis	Daily
On the ground that	Because
Prior to	Before
Subsequent to	After
The majority of	Most
Until such time as	until

Garner, <u>Legal Writing in Plain English</u> at 40.

In addition, do not quote poetry or literature, quote the <u>law</u> and <u>cite</u> to it properly. See the following table for proper citation forms and the corresponding Bluebook section.

Cases	*State v. Thompson,* 123 N.C. App. 234, 234 S.E.2d 56 (2004).	Rule 10
	In re A.B., 341 N.C. 29, 121 S.E.2d 456 (2001).	
Short form	*Thompson,* 123 N.C. App. at 242, 234 S.E.2d at 60. **OR** *Id.* at 242, 234 S.E.2d at 60.	
Statutes	N.C. Gen. Stat. § 7B-1100 (2005)	Rule 12
Short form	Section 7B-1100 **OR** N.C. Gen. Stat. § 7B-1100.	
Constitutions	N.C. Const. art. XIV, § 2.	Rule 11
Legislative materials	N.C. Sess. Laws 2005-384.	Rule 13
Books	Debra Jones, The Law and Me 32 (1992).	Rule 15
Law reviews	Patrice David, *Guardians ad Litem: The Unsung Heroes,* 104 N.C. L. Rev. 28 (1999).	Rule 16

Do not use legalese or Latin terms because they tend to slow down a reader's progress and make a brief more difficult to read. Do not make a judge's law clerk look up the meaning of some obscure Latin phrase! For example: Use terms such as "*inter alia*" only when you have already used the phrase "among other things." Use terms such as: therefore; thus; heretofore; herein; hereinabove; wherein; etc. sparingly. Increase your use of transitions for better flow. Use "therefore" <u>only</u> when you are trying to draw attention to an important conclusion.

Keep it <u>concise</u>. You should use sentences and paragraphs sparingly. Do not repeat yourself. If you can adequately respond to a 35 page appellant's brief in 10 pages, the judge will appreciate it! **Know when to stop writing**: Some of the best legal writing is the shortest! Stop when you have said all you need to say in a clear and concise manner that keeps the reader interested because judges are busy people. We attorneys tend to ramble on because we believe that repeating sometime a thousand times will get our point across. Repetition may work during an oral argument, but in legal writing, it is quite different. (It is no accident that the N.C. Rules of Appellate Procedure limit the number of pages in a brief.)

<u>Convey</u> your points effectively. Specifically ask the court for what you want. Use active voice. Tell a compelling story. Argue your strongest points first. Use section titles to argue your case. Refrain from repeating the appellant. Similar to oral arguments, show the appellate court <u>why</u> the trial court was (in)correct in its holding, tell the appellate court exactly how the opinion should be written and then make the court feel good about its decision.

In other words, find an analogous case that has similar facts to your own. Draw analogies between the two cases and argue that the court should hold the same way in your case as it did in the analogous case. Then explain why the analogous case was such a good holding. Point to any other holdings that came out of the case you are citing.

Check **your work.** And double check your work! The best way to proofread is by reading the finished product aloud. Remember to confirm that your citations are correct. Cite to both North Carolina and Southeastern reporters. Make sure all page numbers are correct. Use short cites where appropriate. Put 50 words or more in a block quote. Remember to cite to pages of the transcript and the record. Also, remember that you may only use 12-point font in Courier or Courier New. If you are using Times New Roman, you must use 14-point font. *See* N.C. R. App. P. 28(j)(1)(B).

Grammar

Write in active voice. Active voice writing changes the focus of your sentence and gives it more power. Classic example: "The ball was thrown by John." Where is the focus? On the ball, not John. Instead, use "John threw the ball."

Examples of passive voice: (1) The accident was caused by the defendant; (2) The defendant was heard to say he was sorry. Instead, use (1) The defendant caused the accident; and (2) She heard the defendant say he was sorry. On rare occasions, you may want to use passive voice, but use it sparingly. You may want to use it if you do not know who took the action.

Use proper punctuation! Use commas where you have coordinating conjunctions such as "and, but, or, for, yet," and the conjunction is connecting two <u>independent</u> clauses. To determine if a clause is independent, ask yourself if it can stand on its own. For example, "Bob went to the Post Office, and he mailed his letters." Both phrases can stand on its own, so a comma is appropriate here.

However, do not overuse commas. Read the sentence out loud and consider placing commas where you would naturally pause in reading the sentence. Conversely, read a sentence you have written, pausing at the commas, and listen to whether the sentence sounds natural. When in doubt, read the sentence to someone else.

Know when to use semi-colons for additional punch. One example is to use a semi-colon to link independent phrases without a conjunction. Example: Mary went to the back; she withdrew money. This example stresses the second phrase a bit. Another example: "Mary was depressed and she cried every night.." or "Mary was depressed; she cried every night."

Additionally, use semi-colons to divide items in a list following a colon, which is used a great deal in legal writing. Example: "The Court held that: (1) Plaintiff failed to state a prima facie case of retaliation; (2) Defendants did not violate Title VII in terminating Plaintiff's employment; and (3) plaintiff was not entitled to damages."

Quotation marks. Punctuation usually goes <u>inside</u> quotation marks, even where the punctuation is not part of the original quote. Exceptions are semi-colons and colons, which can be placed in brackets. Remember: If you are going to change capitalization in a quote, be sure to bracket the letter.

In subject/verb agreement, the subject of the sentence and the subject's verb must agree. Examples: **Joan is** willing to fight this all the way to the Supreme Court. **Joan and John are** willing to fight this all the way to the Supreme Court. *Note: The use of "nor" and "or" between subjects in a sentence is tricky. They both give you a singular subject unless one of the subjects is already plural. Example: (1) "Neither John nor Joan <u>is willing</u> to fight this all the way to the Supreme Court." (2) "Neither Joan nor her friends <u>are willing</u> to fight this all the way to the Supreme Court."

A few pointers on plural as opposed to singular subjects: (a) "The court" is singular; (b) "The jury" is singular, as in "The jury returned a verdict;" and (c) "The jurors" is plural. Remember: Do not confuse possessives with plurals! Differentiate between "the attorneys" and "the attorney's…"

In addition, do not mix up "its" and "it's." Attorneys often get this wrong! "Its" is the possessive form of "it." (This is one of the few cases where the possessive is not made by adding an apostrophe). "It's" is the contraction for "it is." Also remember that "judgment" only has only one "e."

Every word you write in your brief is another opportunity to persuade the court of your position. In that vein, use headings to your advantage. Often appellants' briefs are disorganized and hard to follow. Therefore, make your brief that much more understandable and easy to follow by dividing the arguments cleanly. Use headings to advocate your position, rather than just restating the appellant's headings.

Subdivide headings if necessary for multiple arguments. Explain <u>why</u> the court should hold in your favor. For example:

```
The trial court did not err in finding B.R. to be a
neglected child.
                    versus

     The trial court correctly found that B.R. was a
neglected child because it found clear and convincing
evidence that B.R.'s parents failed to adequately provide for
her medical needs.
```

Tell a compelling story. This is the area in which the attorney can really shine! Tell the court about the "good stuff," as a result of a prior trial court determination. Remind the court of how it was before the appeal process began.

Consider conveying sympathy for the other side. This helps the court realize that you understand the difficulty courts face in making some of their decisions. However, always return to the needs of your client and stress that the scales should tip in favor of your client and why.

Most importantly, finish your brief ON TIME!

Consider electronically filing your brief.

Want to speed up the appeals process? Consider signing up for electronic filing at http://www.ncappellatecourts.org/nc_main_1.nsf. This service will allow you to submit documents electronically to the NC Court of Appeals and Supreme Court at any time of the day or night.

In order to participate in the online filing process, you will need: (1) access to a computer; (2) internet access; (3) adobe acrobat; and (4) access to a scanner for attachments (if any). If you have the prerequisites on hand, head to the site listed above, and apply to participate in online filing. Within a day or two of applying, you will receive a notice confirming your registration. After that, you're good to go!

Once you log into the e-filing website, you will be prompted to type in your user ID and password, and then information regarding the particular case the submission is regarding, names of counsel of record, etc. Finally, you will be prompted to upload your document in PDF format. After you have submitted the document, you will be able to print out a record of your transaction. You should continue to serve all documents on counsel of record by mail, even if filing electronically.

For more detailed information about e-filing in North Carolina, go to: http://www.aoc.state.nc.us/www/public/sc/suggestcoa.htm.

APPENDIX F: SAMPLE BRIEF

No. COA08-197   TWENTY-NINTH JUDICIAL DISTRICT

NORTH CAROLINA COURT OF APPEALS

* *

IN THE MATTER OF:)
)
)   <u>From Polk County</u>
    S.A.,   )   05 JA 456
    Minor child.   )

* *

BRIEF ON BEHALF OF THE MINOR CHILD BY
APPELLEE GUARDIAN AD LITEM

* *

<u>INDEX</u>

TABLE OF AUTHORITIES

CASE LAW:

STATUTES:

STATEMENT OF THE CASE

On 20 August 2003, the Polk County DSS filed a juvenile petition alleging that Sally was abused, neglected and dependent. (R.p.3-5) On 21 November 2007, the trial court terminated Respondent Father's parental rights to Sally. (R.p.202) Respondent Father appeals to this Court. (R.p.210)

STATEMENT OF THE FACTS

DSS has been involved with this family since 1992. (R.p.7) Respondent Father entered into a case plan with DSS in September 2003, in which he was to: (1) maintain a drug-free lifestyle; (2) have a substance abuse assessment; (3) follow the recommendations after the assessment; (4) develop relationships with people who are not engaged in criminal activity; (5) maintain employment; (6) have random drug tests; and (7) have random visits to his home by DSS. (T.p.14)

Sally was first adjudicated abused, neglected and dependent in October 2003. Respondent Father has been convicted of: (1) misdemeanor possession of illegal drugs; (2) three counts of possession of drug paraphernalia; (3) three counts of possession of marijuana; (4) hit and run; and (5) two counts of operating a vehicle with no insurance. Further facts will be developed below.

ARGUMENT

I. FINDING OF FACT 34 IS SUPPORTED BY CLEAR, COGENT AND CONVINCING EVIDENCE.

The trial court must make findings of fact which are supported by this evidentiary standard, and the findings of fact must support the trial court's conclusions of law. *In re Shermer*, 156 N.C. App. 281, 285, 576 S.E.2d 403, 406 (2003).

Finding of fact 34 provides the following: "The DSS and GAL Court Reports as contained in the file of this matter were received into evidence in support of this disposition and the matters therein and opinions concerning the best interest of the child are adopted and incorporated herein." (R.p.206) Respondent Father contends that he disputes this finding of fact, which is curious, since it does not mention him at all. This finding of fact only states that the DSS and GAL reports were received into evidence and that the trial court incorporated the opinions of those reports into the order. Respondent Father offers no legal argument why this finding of fact is disputed. Accordingly, this argument should be deemed abandoned pursuant to Rule 28(b)(6) of the N.C. Rules of Appellate Procedure. *See* N.C. R. App. P. 28(b)(6) (2008).

II. THE TRIAL COURT PROPERLY CONCLUDED THAT THE CHILD WAS A NEGLECTED AND DEPENDENT JUVENILE.

After October 2005, Respondent Father never visited with Sally or even requested visits. He only went to one PPAT meeting. (T.p.16) He did not keep in contact with Sally, or send her gifts or letters, except for Christmas 2005. (T.p.17) However, when he brought these presents, he did not even ask about Sally's status or well-being. (T.p.17)

At the time of the hearing, Respondent Father was serving another prison sentence. He also had pending drug and weapon charges against him. These offenses were all committed from July 2005 to April 2007. He has a lengthy rap sheet, which includes violent crimes. (R.p.241-55) Additionally, Respondent Father's live-in girlfriend also had a history of recent violent crimes. (R.p.98,294-95) Ms. Edwards testified that Sally told her that when policemen came to the door of Respondent Father, she was told to hide under the bed. (T.p.35-37) She also indicated that Respondent Father would also hide when police knocked at his door. (T.p.37)

Moreover, Respondent Father has not been able to stay clean. (T.p.26) He cooperated with random drug screens. (T.p.33) But, of sixteen drug tests, thirteen were positive. (T.p.62, R.p.298-314)

Lastly, because Respondent Father has been unable to remain

clean and has not completed his case plan, he willfully left Sally in foster care for more than twelve months without showing the trial court that reasonable progress has been made in correcting the circumstances that led to Sally's removal.

CONCLUSION

Contrary to Respondent Father's claim, the trial court's order is proper. The undersigned respectfully requests that the Court of Appeals uphold the trial court's determinations.

Respectfully submitted, this the _____ day of _____.

_____

Name
Bar Number
Address
Telephone Number
Facsimile Number
Email Address
Attorney for ENTER PARTY'S NAME

WORD COUNT CERTIFICATION

This brief is submitted in proportional type (Times New Roman, 14 point font). This brief contains 4,720 words, which is not more than the 8,750 words allowed by N.C. R. App. P. 28(j).

APPENDIX F: TIPS FOR ORAL ARGUMENTS

Most cases will not be orally argued before the Court of Appeals. Juvenile matters are never orally argued. If you get a case to the Supreme Court, however, an oral argument is customary. The purposes of oral argument are to: (a) clarify the issues and facts on appeal; (b) explain the scope of the issues; and (c) discuss the logical and practical effects of the law and facts. While arguing, you should note the following tips:

DO the following:

- Arrive on time
- Dress appropriately in professional attire
- Do not read from your notes, brief or record on appeal
- Have a concise outline
- Motivate the judges to view the case sympathetically
- Simplify the information
- Answer all questions posed by the court, but only after thinking them through
- Make a positive impression
- Demonstrate that your argument will stand under fire
- Refer the panel to specific pages in the record or transcript
- Speak slowly and clearly
- Make sure that you have signed the brief

DO NOT do the following:
- Exaggerate
- Use an inappropriate tone of voice (shouting or mumbling)
- Delay while looking for something in your notes
- Display lack of respect toward the bench
- Re-argue facts
- Refer to matters outside the record
- Fail to listen carefully to the court's questions (and answer a question that has not been asked)
- Move around or postpone answering a question

APPENDIX G: APPEAL INFORMATION SHEET

See Form COA-81 on www.nccourts.org for a .pdf fillable form.

Frequently Asked Questions

1. I have filed a notice of appeal in my client's civil case. What do I need to do next?

      Civil appeals are discussed in **Rule 3**. After filing a written notice of appeal within 30 days of the entry of the order, make sure to arrange for a transcript of the proceedings (**Rule 7**). You have 14 days after the notice of appeal is filed to file the transcript arrangement with the trial clerk of court. Serve the notice and transcript arrangement on all parties. (See **Rule 7(a)(1)**).

2. I need to file a Proposed Record on Appeal. What should I include?

      Records on appeal are governed by **Rule 9**. A proposed record on appeal should include all relevant orders filed during the pendency of the case, including the pleadings and notice of appeal. It should also include documents that are at issue. For example, if there is a contract dispute, a copy of the actual contract should be included in the proposed record on appeal. Additionally, exhibits admitted at trial should be included if not too voluminous. Relevant filings from an underlying case may also be included. Additionally, you should include documents listed in **Rule 9(a)(1)**: (a) index; (b) identification statement regarding the judge, trial court district and session; (c) summons; (d) pleadings; (e) evidence presented at trial; (f) transcript of jury instructions, if at issue; (g) issues submitted to the jury and verdict sheet; (h) judgment or order that is being appealed; (i) notice of appeal; (j) documents filed in proceedings; (k) assignments of error; (l) statement on whether the proceedings were recorded by an electronic device; and (m) statement regarding a supplement to the record on appeal, if applicable. See **Rules 9(a)(2)** and **9(a)(3)** for the record on appeal for administrative and criminal appeals.

3. How do I know if the opposing side included everything I need in the Proposed Record on Appeal?

      Look through your copy of the file. Make sure all of the items in **Rule 9(a)(1)** are included. (See #2 above) If anything is missing, you may object and/or amend the record on appeal within 30 days. Additionally, you can file a supplement to the Record on Appeal, which would probably be more convenient for all of the parties.

4. Will the Court of Appeals allow me to include a document after the Record has been settled?

Most of the time. You may always file a Motion to Amend the Record on Appeal all the way up to the actual hearing of the appeal. (See Rule 37).

5.   How do I know when my case will be argued and whether it will be decided on the briefs or oral argument?

Rule 30 concerns oral arguments and unpublished opinions. Both the Court of Appeals and the Supreme Court will mail and email an argument schedule a few weeks before the argument will be heard. All juvenile appeals taken pursuant to Rule 3.1 do not have oral arguments and are decided solely on the briefs. The appellate court may unilaterally decide to consider the case solely on the briefs. In that case, the court will send notification to the attorney, informing her not to appear. Generally, all Supreme Court cases are argued.

6.   How long do the appellate courts have to decide my appeal?

As long as they want. There is no authority mandating that either court file an opinion within a certain amount of time. Nonetheless, the courts have an informal rule to have cases disposed of within three to six months after the oral argument.

7.   I need to file an appeal, but the time to do so has passed. What should I do?

File a writ of *certiorari* pursuant to Rule 21.

8.   May I withdraw from an appeal after the notice of appeal has been filed and before the opinion has come down?

Yes, but your Motion to Withdraw must include your reasons for the withdrawal. (See Rule 37(d)-(f)).

9.   May I include non-stamp-filed documents in the Record on Appeal?

Yes, but opposing counsel may object to the inclusion of the document.

10.   Do I include the transcript in the Record on Appeal?

The transcript is considered part of the Record on Appeal; however, it should be mailed separately from the Record on Appeal. This included transcripts from depositions.

11.   When can I cite to an unpublished opinion in my brief?

Only when you cannot find a published opinion on point. If you include an unpublished opinion, you must attach a copy of it to your brief. Remember, an unpublished decision is not considered legal authority, so you would not want to base your entire argument on a holding in an unpublished case. (See Rule 30(e)).

12.   When should I attach an appendix to my brief?

Appendices are covered in Rule 28. Appendices in an appellant's brief are required where specific portions of the transcript need to be reproduced verbatim. You must also include any relevant portion of a document needed to understand the arguments at issue. Appendices in an appellee's brief are mandatory where the appellee presents a new or additional question, which need verbatim transcript pages to be understood. (See Rule 28(d)).

13.   Should I concede any arguments in my brief? Oral argument?

Yes. If your argument is clearly contrary to established legal authority and you cannot make a public policy argument, do not waste the court's time. Concede the point.

14.   When may I file a Motion to Dismiss an appeal?

At any time after the Notice of Appeal has been filed. If the Record on Appeal has not yet been docketed in the Court of Appeals, file the motion to dismiss at the trial court. If the record on appeal has been docketed (and given a docket number), file it at the appellate court.

15.   How far in advance may I file a Motion for Extension of Time to Complete the Record on Appeal/Transcript/Brief?

As soon as you realize you will need it. Motions for extensions of time are disfavored, so if you believe you are running out of time, file the extension motion and point out that the time to have the record/transcript/brief has not yet passed. Be sure to include a good reason. (See Rule 37).

INDEX